IMPACT
ENTREPRENEUR

It starts
with a Step!

Mike + Kelly Ohm

See Ch. 10

15+ ENTREPRENEURS SHARE INSIGHTS & SECRETS FOR BUILDING A BUSINESS WITH PURPOSE & MEANING

IMPACT
ENTREPRENEUR

WENDI BLUM WEISS &
PATRICIA WOOSTER

Impact Entrepreneur: 15+ Entrepreneurs Share Insights & Secrets For Building a Business With Purpose & Meaning

WosterMedia LLC
Tampa, Florida
woostermediabooks.com

ISBN: 979-8-9861607-7-1

Published by WoosterMedia LLC
woostermediabooks.com

WoosterMedia

TABLE OF CONTENTS

INTRODUCTION

The World's Wake Up Call

There are major life events that completely change the landscape of how we live, what we will tolerate, and how we choose to navigate our careers.

In 2020, the whole world shut down as the spread of COVID forced people indoors and into a new reality for several years. Individuals and families who were used to the hurried pace of busy mornings, school drop-offs, morning work commutes, long hours, and a full evening of kid's activities and preparation to start the entire process the next day were now forced to pause. For the first time in many people's adult lives they were home and had free time.

We learned something very important about ourselves during this time—we were exhausted and tired of the hustle and grind of jam-packed schedules. Having no time to do the things that were most meaningful, like simply taking a walk around the neighborhood, working on a home project, or calling a friend just to check up on how they were doing left us frustrated and feeling empty. We were tired of climbing the corporate ladder, overworking and hoping someday our time would come when we could retire.

Since then people have woken up to the unpredictability and shortness of life. Unwilling to settle on low job satisfaction, there has been a huge shift and surge of people starting businesses or entrepreneurship. A new record was set in America with five million new business applications filed by first-time entrepreneurs. Many people discovered during their mandated pause they wanted to reconsider how and where they were willing to spend their time in a post-pandemic world. No longer tolerating subpar, they decided it was time to be proactive and create their life by design while they are still youthful enough to enjoy it. Hence the birth of intentional living and doing meaningful work that matters.

Birth of the Impact Entrepreneur

Some people start a business or become an entrepreneur because they have a mission or a cause they are passionate about, many times inspired by a personal story that drives them. Others feel called to fulfill a life purpose or leave a legacy that extends beyond their mortality.

One thing all of these ideas have in common is that a solopreneur, company, or business is built around a vision of making the world a better place by solving a problem, making something better, and most importantly, impacting people favorably.

All of the aforementioned factors make an impact entrepreneur enthusiastic, passionate, and eager to jump out of bed in the morning to share their expertise and genius with as many people as they can and as often as they can. Think about it: when we lean into and share our gifts and talents, we can't help but impact our clients. Work is no longer an obligation and becomes a privilege to share, help, and serve others. When we lead from a place of service, we feel fulfilled and are grateful to do meaningful work that we love, and everyone wins.

What you will discover in this book is that an impact entrepreneur is not about a specific type of work or occupation. It's about how each of these entrepreneurs shows up in the world and how they feel when they are doing their best work and creating a difference in people's lives. As you read their stories, notice how winding their journey was to get to where they are today. Every experience and every challenge served as a lesson. No obstacle, such as education, experience, finances, or age, stopped them from pursuing their ultimate purpose.

It is our greatest hope and wish that the stories in this book inspire you to live your life by design. Perhaps there is a change in career also out there for you, too. There's never been a better time to start a business, build a community, and live your life with purpose and passion.

May you create an impact following your passion.

Wendi Blum Weiss & Patricia Wooster

I BELIEVE IN AND PROMOTE THE IDEA THAT EVERYONE HAS THE POWER TO CREATE THE LIFE THEY DESIRE.

Wendi Blum Weiss

CHAPTER 1

THE UNFORESEEN GIFT OF LOSING EVERYTHING
BY WENDI BLUM WEISS

The first time I lost all of my possessions I was 17. My brother and I waited every day for the moving van to arrive. Crickets. Nothing. Nada. Two months went by before I remembered the one thing we did take with us on our move from Rhode Island to South Florida: the Yellow Pages. On this particular day, I decided to start calling around to see if I could find the company our single, overworked mom had used to pack up our belongings. First call, nothing. Second one, the same. But on the third call, bingo. The man who answered the phone knew immediately who I was when I inquired if they were the ones who packed us up.

He bluntly replied, "Your stuff was auctioned off more than a month ago."

In disbelief, I responded, "Are you kidding me? How can we get our stuff back?"

His quick retort was a cold dose of reality. "It's too late; everything is gone," he replied. "At this point, unfortunately, there isn't anything anyone can do."

I was stunned. My brother was heartbroken. As an avid athlete, all of his trophies were in that van. For me, it was all the photos I had collected growing up. Devastated, we realized everything we owned was gone in an instant.

When our mom came home from her waitress job that night, I confronted her with the details of the call. Her response was unexpected and bizarre. "Pretend there was a fire, and you lost everything," she said. Then, she turned and walked out of the room, downplaying the whole thing. Her body language made it abundantly clear that the subject was not to be brought up again; it was now closed.

Years later, I've come to understand the tremendous strain our mom must have been under, particularly the financial burden of being unable to pay our moving bill. However, back then it was a lot for two teenagers to process. That day was a turning point for me and impacted the trajectory of my life. The experience strengthened my determination to stand on my own two feet: to move out, finance my own education, earn my own money, succeed on my own terms, and navigate life without relying on others. So that is exactly what I did.

The next time I said goodbye to all of my possessions, I was 47. By then I had navigated 30 years of work life, put myself through college, graduated with a finance degree, and built a strong track record in sales with three Fortune 500 companies: Pitney Bowes, Dictaphone, and Panasonic. Then I moved into the pharmaceutical industry, crossed over the $200K a year threshold, won awards, had a nice expense account, and was fully immersed in corporate culture.

By this time, I had accumulated many beautiful things, including a five-bedroom home and a lot of designer furnishings. What was different this go-round was that it was by choice that I decided to give away most of our home's interior belongings. It was a tough year for many people, who were losing their houses to foreclosure due to the mortgage crisis in 2008. Banks were faltering. The economy was redefining itself, and so was I.

Labels, Identity, and Reinvention

As I was giving away my adorned treasures, I was also unraveling and shifting my identity. *"Who was I?"* I knew I wasn't my belongings or stuff. *"Who am I?"* I was someone who was re-evaluating her life.

"Who do I want to become?" I wasn't sure but was leaning into a whole new world of possibility that revolved around entrepreneurship.

First, I wanted to decipher my multiple social, professional, and personal identities, roles, and the labels. I was undeniably a mom, daughter, sister, wife, and so forth. I was also a college grad with a finance degree, an award-winning salesperson, corporate leader, sales manager, and rule follower, while at the same time acknowledging that many years prior I had been a struggling teenager, a waitress, a bartender, a complete rebel, someone who used drugs, and a total rule breaker.

There were certainly crossroads where my life could have gone in any direction. Approaching the age of 50, I was now deciding what the second half of my life was going to look like. Losing all of my possessions the first time around gave me the drive to redirect my misfortunes into building a successful career and having a strong work ethic. When I gave my possessions away the second time, I was taking a stand for something different: owning my freedom, flexibility, and reinventing myself.

Saying Goodbye to Corporate

The writing was on the wall: it was becoming apparent that I was not only saying goodbye to a house and a marriage but leaving my two-decade career in the pharmaceutical industry.

The number one question on my mind was, "If I jump ship from corporate to entrepreneurship, will I still be able to sustain myself at the level at which I am accustomed?" My kids were in college, and my livelihood needed to be the backbone to hold all of the pieces of my life together.

I had two voices battling it out: one that was afraid to leave and urged me to play it safe and the other one believed in me and thankfully, eventually won out. I would be remiss not to mention here how hard this decision was for me to make, and it did not happen overnight. It was a grueling process and without hiring a badass business coach to whom I paid substantial money, I don't know if I would have had the guts to do it on my own.

One year later, I created an LLC and was now officially the CEO of Success Blueprint. By claiming it and naming it, my new identity became real. I was officially an entrepreneur!

The Seduction of the Side Hustle

Entrepreneurship wasn't an entirely foreign concept to me. Growing up in financially constrained circumstances, I was constantly devising ways to earn my own money. In college, I worked 25+ hours a week for four years at Publix to pay my tuition and room and board. But that wasn't all; I also took on side jobs, including cleaning and painting houses, to earn extra income.

Post-college, as I began my career as a financial analyst, I continued to pursue a weekend side hustle. My roommate and I proudly printed business cards and named our company "Walls of Distinction." We specialized in wallpapering and painting new houses for a local builder during the weekends.

After my first son was born, I started a baby clothing line and thoroughly enjoyed networking with other moms, selling the hand-painted baby outfits at local preschools. This venture wasn't highly profitable; however, I really enjoyed the camaraderie of being with my new peer group of fellow moms.

Lastly, during my long tenure in the pharmaceutical industry, I tested out a number of health-related side hustles to satisfy my insatiable thirst for health, fitness, and longevity. For one year, I became a partner in a fitness apparel and spin studio, an experience that was both physically exhausting and exhilarating. I also taught yoga, led meditation workshops, and organized numerous retreats to destinations like Bali, Costa Rica, and Colorado. These experiences immersed me in a world I hadn't anticipated would be so deep and meaningful. Involvement with these pursuits also ignited my passion for writing, eventually leading me to become an author and publish my very first book about designing a life you love.

Resigning

At this point, I am constantly rehearsing my resignation, fully aware that leaving won't be easy. Saying goodbye to a six-figure income, to colleagues I respect, and to a reliable career that had been on autopilot—one that helped me raise my family early on as a single mom—was daunting. Yet, a profound mission erupted in my heart, a deep calling to serve humanity in a different way. I often imagined being 90 years old on my deathbed, feeling proud for having taken this leap of faith.

I vividly envisioned a future where I was no longer a sales executive wearing pearls and a navy blue suit at a $96 billion-dollar company with 34,000 employees. I saw a future without endless meetings, stringent FDA regulations, or the external pressures of the corporate grind.

Instead I saw myself as a world-class leader, well-dressed in my own distinctive style, now as an innovator, an advocate for good in the world, and a guide for those aspiring to unleash their greatness. Many of these individuals, like myself, transitioned from corporate careers to following their true calling.

I established my brand, declaring myself as the success and strategy coach. To solidify my commitment further, I listed all the reasons why this was important to me and crafted my meaningful mission statement: "To empower men and women to step into their brilliance, unleash their unique superpowers and make a positive impact in the world." I placed one copy on my bedroom nightstand and another in my home office, serving as daily reminders of my purpose and ambition.

Now, as I was about to turn 50, I decided that the best birthday present I could give myself would be full permission to take off the golden handcuffs that kept me bound to the corporate world as my only lifetime career. When my birthday arrived, I kept my promise: I turned in my resignation and gifted myself this extraordinary new beginning.

Authority, Credibility, and Standing Out: Becoming a Speaker and Best-Selling Author

Starting out in a new career at the age of 50 comes with a dilemma. How could I maximize my efforts and condense ten years' worth of work to become known as a leader and expert in a brand-new industry in just one year?

There were two popular ways to speed up the process: write a book and become a public speaker.

Here is what I discovered:

1. **Establishing Authority**: You stand out online and instantly have clout.
2. **Expanding Reach**: You go from one-to-one to a much bigger audience of one-to-many.
3. **Accelerated Learning**: You shorten the learning curve, can test out your material, and get immediate feedback.

I rolled up my sleeves and jumped on this idea right out of the gate. First, I published a book and added author to my official title and upgraded my identity. Being a published author meant I also had a book as my first product to sell. So I set up a table at churches, temples, schools, organizations, and wellness events to do just that. Most importantly, I was meeting people and collecting emails. This was key! Many entrepreneurs are slackers when it comes to collecting contact information and putting it into a database.

Next, I came up with a couple of enticing talk titles and offered to speak for free. Sometimes, I was even willing to pay to speak as well, for example, when I flew to Toronto and presented on "3 Mistakes Entrepreneurs Make When They Launch Their Business." That day, I addressed a group of 300 newly established business owners and walked out with 12 brand-new clients. Being willing to invest to get in front of the right audience proved to be a huge advantage. This was a milestone moment, significantly gaining momentum in my first year of business. It's a rite of passage to becoming a future paid speaker.

Little did I know that a decade later, I would be helping entrepreneurs become best-selling co-authors and public speakers like the writers in this book.

Referrals, Clients, and Growing Your Income

The very first client of mine was referred to me by one of the top doctors I used to call on at Jackson Memorial Hospital. He used to listen to Tony Robbins' CDs and greatly appreciated my new line of work.

The patient had been in the hospital for three weeks, and her doctor highly encouraged her to meet with me to redefine her mindset. The first meeting was a bit awkward. I drove to her house and sat in the driveway for 20 minutes before going up to knock on the door. When I finally did, she looked at me with suspicion and asked, "Why were you sitting in my driveway so long?" I replied, "I was setting an intention to provide you with the very best possible outcome of our time together." Truth be told, I was also very nervous—this was my very first client. My honest response seemed to open her up for our very first session.

We sat down and she proceeded to hand me $500 in cash for our sessions together. I was, again, so uncomfortable. I didn't know what to do with it. I had never received money in this kind of way before. It felt so strange. For 40 years, my salary was deposited directly into my bank account. My identity shifted once again to redefine my new normal.

The money conversation can be the most awkward stage of starting to work for yourself, especially for someone coming from a J.O.B or the corporate world. It's a whole new paradigm, and your entire identity around money has to shift.

Impact

The clients I work with are heart centered, mission driven, and want to make a positive impact in the world. I've been intentional about working with people who are all of those things. Luckily enough, when you work for yourself, you get to choose where you put your focus and who you want to work with.

There is one dilemma that comes with the territory; impact entrepreneurs are so generous, and the issues that come up are twofold. They often have a tendency to over give to the level of exhaustion. Secondly, they feel guilty to own their value and charge what they are worth.

Moreover, even today I am astonished to see how often new entrepreneurs give their products and services away for free, especially in the coaching field. It is the opposite in the corporate world. Many salaried employees feel entitled to more money and secondly, only give to the level of what is expected and rarely more.

So how do you strike a balance between impact and money as an entrepreneur? I believe they are two sides of the same coin, and impact and money are actually allies. I also believe you have to give yourself full permission to be motivated by both because frankly, the more money you make, the more impact you can have in the world.

There is a delicate balance when you first start out working for yourself, especially when you are motivated by a strong desire to give, share, serve, and make a difference. It makes sense to give people a taste of your product or service by offering them something free. I myself give away all sorts of freebies: an e-book on *Success Strategies to Launch Your Business,* a speaker's one sheet to use to get booked on stages and podcasts, and a weekly Shine Your Mojo Conference Call. Doing so puts goodwill out into the ethers. After you do so, you've earned the right to share your core product or offer. The free version gives your prospective client an opportunity to try you out before buying. Makes sense, right? Also, along the way, you are helping people and impacting lives.

I really like this model that is often used in the coaching field. It also applies to other industries as well, for example, food tastings at supermarkets, test driving a car at the dealership, and so on.

AS AN ENTREPRENEUR, MOST OF THE TIME YOU HAVE TO MAKE YOUR OWN WAY STARTING FROM ZERO.

Looking back now to my younger years, being able to start something from nothing was an unforeseen gift by losing everything at age 17, and learning how to make it on my own was an invaluable skill to master early on.

Trial and Error

Entrepreneurship is far from an exact science. Instead, it resembles a path marked by trial and error. Countless tales exist of individuals who have ventured into various business endeavors, only to meet failure head-on. While we often hear about instant success stories, what's commonly overlooked is the reality that these achievements often result from years of experimentation, learning from mistakes, and ultimately finding a formula that succeeds.

It could be the reason entrepreneurs try so many different avenues before they hit it big. Over the years, I tested out a number of creative endeavors on the side while I worked in the corporate world. I taught fitness classes. I produced weekend wellness retreats. I created and sold inspirational tee-shirts. I even wrote my first book. I did all this while still working a full-time job. Doing so combined my passions and fulfilled me while testing out all of these extra income producing ideas to see if I could gain traction.

The beauty of entrepreneurship is how interconnected it is with growing as a human being. We grow so much when we treat life like a big experiment and explore different interests. Every creative project I took on and side hustle I participated in, offered a fresh new way to look at the world. Sometimes things didn't work out the way I wanted them to; however, I felt empowered just by trying. It gave me the stamina and the courage to try again in a different way with the knowledge that comes from experience.

It took me many years to learn email marketing, build out funnels, and embrace technology. I'm not entirely there yet, but I'm getting better every year. You've got to be in the game to win the game. And this game is worth winning if the spark of entrepreneurship is inside of you.

If you want to become an impact entrepreneur or change your life in any way, shape, or form with the right mentoring, mindset, and planning, it's possible. It's what drives me every day.

What advice would you give somebody looking to enter into entrepreneurship?

When you work for yourself, you have to be a self-starter, which means many times, in the world of entrepreneurship, starting before you are ready.

I remember when I first began creating content online. I knew that if I wanted to establish my business, I needed to do it, but it felt uncomfortable. I kept thinking, "Who am I to be teaching about business, mindset, and designing your life?" I felt like an impostor.

Like many entrepreneurs, I struggled with confidence and redefining my identity. I went from one thing to another, experimenting and testing things out. Many times, I failed. Nevertheless, the one thing I consistently did was stay focused on my desired outcome. By starting before I fully understood what I was doing, I was able to learn while simultaneously taking action. Every time I made a mistake, I would revisit my desired outcome, assess, course-correct, push myself, and keep going.

Also, I realized I needed to cast a wide net, try a lot of things, and see what got traction. Social media is free and gives you immediate feedback in the way of likes, comments, and engagement. If there were crickets, I knew I needed to switch things up. Repetition and consistency are key. Remember, overnight success is rarely overnight. It often takes years of grinding and putting in the hard work.

This is the list I wish someone would have given to me when I first began:

1. Start before you are ready
2. Write out your mission statement, your core principles, values, and vision
3. Hire a business coach who specializes in start-ups
4. Connect with a community
5. Collect emails and put them into a CRM system
6. Become a published author and a public speaker
7. Form partnerships and collaborations
8. Hire someone to handle your administrative work
9. Continuously build and strengthen your skills
10. Create short-form video and be active on social media

What is your ultimate impact?

My heart's ultimate desire centers on meaning and service. I aspire to leave a legacy characterized by good character, a strong work ethic, prioritizing family, nurturing relationships, and living a life dedicated to purpose.

Reflecting on being 17 years old and losing everything, I now see it as a gift in disguise. Looking forward, my drive is to empower my family and help others overcome generational struggles, particularly in areas like self-worth, fear, pain, and financial challenges. Our mom did her best within her abilities, life circumstances, and belief system. I am committed to breaking that cycle and demonstrating that thriving is possible, regardless of heritage, upbringing, age, or current financial status.

Ultimately, my contribution to the world will be through my writings, published books, and work as a motivational speaker. I believe in and promote the idea that everyone has the power to create the life they desire.

How can people connect with you?

You can connect with Wendi Blum Weiss at www.WendiBlum.com and get your free gift at https://linktr.ee/wendiblum

YOU CANNOT CHALLENGE
AND GROW IF YOU ARE
NOT WILLING TO STUMBLE
AROUND A BIT.

Patricia Wooster

CHAPTER 2

THE GIFT OF UNCERTAINTY WHEN PURSUING YOUR DREAMS BY PATRICIA WOOSTER

Two years ago, I was cruising through certainty. I had my daily, weekly, and monthly goals mapped out. I knew approximately when I would retire and where we would live out our golden years. It was a carefully curated and crafted plan that I was 80 percent certain would occur. All we had to do was follow the script, and my husband and I could cruise right into retirement without missing a beat.

Instead, at age fifty, I decided to throw caution to the wind and co-found a software company. This was from the girl who was running a successful publishing company that provided a good income, wonderful clientele, and complete freedom. The same publishing company that had taken me ten years to build. I did this willingly and with little thought. And for an extra bit of risk and excitement, I asked my husband of twenty years to join me and our other cofounder to be the third business partner.

Welcome to my midlife crisis.

The timing was perfect to move from total occupational and financial security to complete uncertainty. I had several inflection points that may have contributed to what many saw as a rash and uncharacteristic decision:

- My oldest son left for college.
- We were exiting a global pandemic.

- Retirement plans were safely secured.
- My current career was easy for me, and I love a challenge.
- And that first gray hair that my hairdresser likes to call "tinsel."

I jumped in with both feet, and together with my two business partners, we built the first personalized employee engagement system for human resources. Mind you, none of us had ever spent a day working in human resources ourselves. But we were all wildly committed to making a difference in how people view and experience their time at work. As three founders in their 50s, we had all contributed a significant amount of our lifetime to working and understood the challenges and issues that arose between employees, managers, and companies. This was particularly timely as the pandemic exposed many of those issues and added a few dozen more. Work environments were changing as people transitioned from office environments to remote workers and then added hybrid to the mix after restrictions were lifted. It felt like a necessary and exciting time to create new solutions to match the direction of where companies needed to evolve.

We started our company, Designing Genius, self-funded with plenty of sweat equity. By the end of the first year, we had a handful of investors and a software solution that was ready to release into the marketplace. It has been one of my career's most exciting, challenging, and sometimes scary journeys.

So, how did this shift take place? How did I transition from someone who relied on long-term plans to someone willing to start from scratch? How did I move from risk-averse to one of the most challenging endeavors a person can take (tech start-up founder)? It required an entire switch in mindset and the willingness to shed my current identity. The difference between who I was for the first four decades of my life and who I needed to become was someone okay with uncertainty.

Predictability and certainty are how I've always run my life. My annual planning, daily calendar, and weekly priority lists allow me to create the momentum and progress I desire toward my goals. I need routines and habits to feel safe and grounded. I'm sure this need is based on some childhood trauma or quirk, but it's always been the key driver whenever I've experienced success.

With a business start-up, you have none of those things. There's zero certainty that anyone will like your product. You're operating off of gut instinct, research, and a perceived need for what you are selling. Every day is a never-ending list of things that need to be done without the resources to do them. It's the ability to shift and pivot that keeps most new businesses alive, which is why certainty is not a core characteristic for most entrepreneurs. And it was a very difficult transition for me.

My desire for certainty was overshadowed by my love of freedom that came with this new venture. As business partners, we wanted to create a solution for organizations to address employee disengagement, but we were not set on a particular way to solve the problem. This gave us the freedom to brainstorm, talk to a lot of people, and innovate as we gathered information. We had to be okay with scrapping ideas when better ones came along.

I believe this is a huge learning lesson that many entrepreneurs miss. People get stuck on their original idea without validating it. They don't want to give it up because they've already put work into the product, service, marketing, or website. It feels too painful to start over. And I get it. We've changed things thousands of times, and it's time-consuming and feels like you are going backward. But sometimes, you must take two steps back before taking a gigantic leap forward.

It's particularly difficult when the thing you are letting go of is good but not a great fit for what you are trying to accomplish. I have started and killed off so many projects that I have lost count. It gets a little bit easier every time, but it is natural to grieve the time and thought that went into the plan that did not work. I suggest giving yourself a mourning period or proper pout and then releasing that idea into the world for someone else to pursue. Then, radically embrace your new idea without looking back. I no longer need certainty because I have witnessed what amazing outcomes follow when you are driven by flow and innovation. It's given me permission to try things without feeling like I need to be 100 percent committed before testing the waters.

Last fall, I decided to pursue a graduate degree in Industrial and Organizational Psychology at Harvard University. I've wanted an advanced degree for years but always made excuses about timing, my commitment, and whether the investment was worth it. I decided to be okay without knowing the answers to those questions. I told my husband and business partner that I would try it, but if the work was too much, I may be done after a semester. In the past, I would have viewed it as a failure to consider quitting something after I started it, but now I value my time and energy too much to continue with activities that no longer serve me.

Luckily, I loved going back to school, and it is of huge value to our software solution and value proposition. I'm able to apply in real-time the concepts I am learning in class to our business. I would never have known this if I hadn't taken a chance. A few months prior to enrolling at Harvard, I signed up for a program that I thought would help with our business, but I quickly realized it was a mistake. Instead of pouring time and energy into it because I was financially committed, I chose to value my time and energy more. I was okay with walking away from it despite my investment. This created the space for me to find a much better fit at Harvard.

I'm finding that the iterations in life are what keep things interesting. My goal is to try as many new things and experiences as possible so that I have no regrets. I don't know if this is a result of me getting older with a bit of "tinsel" in my hair. Or maybe it's a sign of growth as I've reconciled with habits, feelings, and characteristics that kept me stuck and stagnant.

I tell my sons all of the time to just create momentum in their life. Don't worry about too many steps ahead. If you want something, then start moving toward it. Once the movement starts, you'll have greater clarity about the destination. Often, it will involve pit-stops, and sometimes you'll have to turn around, but it's the journey that is the true adventure. It's okay to have the 10-year plan, but don't wrap it in bubble wrap. Be okay with changing it as you and your interests develop and grow.

I truly believe that age is only a number that defines and puts parameters on you if you let it. I have a teenage son who started his entrepreneurial journey in third grade by cleaning and restoring his classmates coveted sneakers. I watched him pivot to selling clothes on eBay and hosting a YouTube channel. Now at age seventeen, he's on his third year as a clothing designer with a successful brand. In a year, he will be heading to Savannah College of Arts and Design to pursue a degree as a fashion designer. We have never let his age stop him from pursuing his interests. I watch in wonderment as he unapologetically puts all of his time and energy into something he loves. I use this as fuel for my own interests. The question I play on repeat is if he's not too young to go after his dreams, then why should I think I am too old to go after mine?

What is the "why" behind what you do?

I wish I could say that my "why" is super profound, but it's not. My joy comes from continuous learning and growth. I am curious to my core. I cannot imagine ever running out of things to learn about. My favorite times in life are when I am really zeroed in on something and on everyday ebbs and flows. Being in the zone is where true genius, innovation, and growth take place, and I'm constantly trying to find ways to put myself there.

My goal is to teach my sons how to find and create this space for themselves. I wish for them to be infinitely curious about anything and everything. Learning and curiosity are independent from age, finances, institutional education, and life circumstances. Watch a toddler for thirty minutes, and you'll witness the wonder that comes with curiosity and exploration. Kids are the masters at being open to trying and experiencing new things, and I'm trying to preserve that in my kids as they now transition into adulthood.

Life is different today than it was for our parents. More and more people are creating lives that allow them to feel the power of living for today. People no longer want to wait for some predetermined milestone in the future to start pursuing their dreams or passions. Whether it's waiting to be done with school, having a certain amount of money in the bank, or retirement, there's always an excuse to put off the joy that can be found today. It's not the monumental pursuits that create the most contentment but the small curiosities that are developed over time that lead to the greatest fulfillment.

What life or business lessons have created the most growth for you?

Lessons learned and growth always come down to *people*. I have learned that different people serve different needs in our lives, and sometimes those are lifelong, and sometimes they are temporary. Oftentimes, I think we believe that one person can serve every need or that if we like someone, we will like them in every area of our lives. This is untrue and unrealistic.

I have incredible friends and family members with whom I could never go into business and amazing business acquaintances who aren't my first social call. I've worked with people who are abrasive and egotistical but incredible at their jobs. And I've had work friends who are terrible workers but the perfect dinner companion. It comes down to knowing a person and where and how they fit into your life.

Years ago, I went into business with a really good friend, and it was fun at first but turned into a disaster. I'm highly organized and like to create project plans and timelines. I want to get tasks and projects done early and efficiently in case of an unforeseen emergency or change. She had a large family and was used to chaos, so she was okay working on projects right up until the deadline. I liked strategy. She liked spontaneity. We quickly discovered that what made us complimentary as friends didn't make us compatible as business partners, so we dissolved the company.

My advice to people who are looking for business partners is to do your homework. Look for someone who has complementary skill sets and a level of expertise you are missing. Discuss roles and responsibilities so you both have a clear understanding of each other's expectations. Consider doing a trial project together to assess each other's working styles, communication, and collaboration. If you decide to move forward and build a business together, create your partnership and operating agreements in the beginning. You can download free or inexpensive contracts online to get started. These agreements outline the intention of your partnership and protect both parties in unforeseeable circumstances. Once it's official, then learn and grow together. Starting a business is exciting but often stressful, so sharing it with someone else can lighten the anxiety while increasing the fun.

What advice would you give to someone considering entrepreneurship?

Think way bigger. Most of us shortchange ourselves and limit how far we can dream. We see successful people and think we are too old, not as well educated, are without resources or not equipped to take on a big challenge. Instead, it's important to address those doubts immediately before they take up space in our heads. Every time I find limiting thoughts intruding, I ask myself, "Why not me? Why can't I be the person who revolutionizes an industry? Why can't I build a company that becomes a legacy for my kids?"

It's the answer to those questions that are important. For example, if the answer is that you think you are too old, then you can start finding evidence of people your age and older who have already accomplished what you want. The evidence for your success is everywhere if you look. People with less, whether finances, resources, expertise, or support have accomplished extraordinary things. Their differentiator is that they believed they could do it, so they pursued it passionately and purposefully.

Once you have that BHAG (big hairy audacious goal), you can start breaking it down into milestones. It's important to note that many of those milestones will change and iterate as your business and understanding of the business evolves, so it's okay to have placeholders. The milestones allow you to create momentum, so as you think about the bigger picture, you're also taking the steps to build the foundation of your business.

The next step is to test your ideas and solution. No one is buying your perfectly designed logo or website, so don't waste the time, energy and resources on those things before you have a proof of concept. The easiest way to test your ideas before potentially building something no one wants is through coaching or consulting. This is an opportunity to deliver massive value to a client while perfecting and crafting your business offer. Most likely the intel you gain during these engagements will make you think about your business and solution differently. So it's a win-win for everyone.

Launching a new business is complicated, with a steep learning curve. Initially, you are the sales representative, product developer, bookkeeper, customer service, and talent. Get some support as soon as you can. Start with mentorship. This can be from your local Small Business Association, a coaching program, or someone you know. Identify where you need guidance and find someone who knows how to do what you lack. This is the most significant shortcut to ramping up your skills and knowledge fast. A great mentor can save you time, energy, and money as you avoid costly mistakes or unnecessary detours.

Finally, take care of yourself. Entrepreneurs will never run out of things they can do for the business, so they need to know when to turn it off and have a personal life. If not, the stress, fatigue, and loneliness will cost them their health, happiness, and well-being in the end. Develop a strong morning and evening routine that includes things like exercise, meditation, gratitude practice, healthy food, and reading. Schedule time away from the office with friends or family members. Connect with other entrepreneurs who understand your stressors and challenges. Make the time to pour into yourself so that you can pour into others through your business.

What is your ultimate impact?

My ultimate impact is to create a legacy that benefits my children and the world they are inheriting. Every decision I make, from the projects I take on and the time and energy I devote to them, must be in alignment with my relationship with my family. I am committed to their growth and development, nurturing them into becoming compassionate and responsible men who will positively impact the world. My husband, Scot, shares the same vision. Together we are building a legacy that prioritizes our sons and their future.

My professional passion is to help people take their expertise and knowledge and share it with others in a meaningful way. Whether it is a corporate professional transitioning into consulting or a former athlete launching their speaking career, I love being the strategist who develops the roadmap with my clients. There are so many people who understand their gifts but don't know how to package and get them into the hands of the right people. Our agency assists with best-selling books, speeches, course creation, and coaching programs. We've also created certification programs and college accredited courses. Anything we can do to help our clients develop solutions around their expertise, we are excited to partner on. If we can deliver that to our clients, then I cannot imagine a greater feeling.

Personally, I want to be known as someone who demonstrates a commitment to their family, friends, and colleagues. I want people to see me as someone who doesn't just surface issues, but solves problems. Sometimes I get it right and other times I fail, and that's okay. You cannot challenge and grow if you are not willing to stumble around a bit. I know with absolute certainty that I have many more failures in front of me as I push myself to take more chances, embrace change, and become more adventurous as I mirror for my sons what it means to create an impact.

How can people connect with you?

I can be found at patriciawooster.com and on LinkedIn @patriciawooster.

I HAVE LONG SUBSCRIBED TO THE BELIEF THAT IF INFORMATION WAS GIVEN TO ME TO DRAMATICALLY IMPROVE MY LIFE, WHO AM I TO KEEP IT TO MYSELF?

Mariana Amilcar

CHAPTER 3

"YOU'RE NOT FAILING; YOU'RE GROWING!" BY MARIANA AMILCAR

The year is 2010. I am 19 years old, and in my second year of college. What a time to be alive! I'm young, energetic, and talented; the world is at my fingertips. I have the drive, resources, and support to do whatever I want with my life. I have examples of success all around me screaming, "You have so much potential! You can be and do anything!" There's one big problem. I have no freaking clue what that's going to be. Here I am studying nursing, a major I sort of fell into, not because of a lifelong dream of being a nurse, but because many of my older friends in the medical field seemed to find work rather quickly after school. So I said, "I guess I'll do that!" The college professors are all saying, "What are you passionate about?" I don't know, hanging out with my friends and watching *The Flavor of Love* on VH1. They say, "Try new things to learn more about yourself, your interests, etc." With what time? I am in school full time, working to pay for school, studying to make it through school, all to end up with a career that I was never really that interested in to begin with. I am stuck. I know in my heart I have to do something different. I feel like time is moving rapidly, and I am lost, going nowhere fast.

This is where most powerful stories begin, right? There's that nagging tug on our hearts that we can't seem to ignore. There's a voice that starts as a whisper, telling us to step out into the unknown, to believe in ourselves, and to have faith, and we bury that voice beneath our doubts, insecurities, and limiting beliefs until that small whisper becomes an overwhelming roar. I was there. And it was just going to take the right person to come into my life at the right time, to help let that voice out. That person was my dad.

For as long as I can remember, my parents worked alongside each other, building an ultimately successful business. They had what many people dream of—a longstanding loving marriage, a successful business, and a beautiful family of eight. That's right. Eight children. All of these things I yearned for (minus the eight kids). I may have lost direction in my life, but I knew what I didn't want. I did not want to work 40+ hours a week in a job I didn't like, to feed a family I hardly get to see, day in and day out for my entire life. I wanted to have a purposeful career. I wanted to impact people's lives in a meaningful way, and I wanted to make a lot of money doing it. I wanted all of this to blend seamlessly with my personal life, where my eventual marriage and family life would flourish. I watched this beautiful example of everything I wanted right in front of my eyes with my parents, so it was no surprise that when my father came to me one day with some unsolicited advice, I listened.

My parents never forced me to or even suggested I join the family business. They simply observed, and when they knew I needed it, they offered. For me, it was simple. I was so miserable with everything I was doing; the thought of doing something new, learning something new, and challenging myself was exhilarating. I looked at an industry that was not only dominated by men, but the average financial advisor was 65 years old. I was neither of those things, and the thought of defying those odds excited me! In other words, I was naive enough to believe I could make it at whatever I tried, so I did just that. I tried.

In my off time between school and my part-time job at the restaurant, I decided I would soak up every bit of knowledge I could from my dad. We would spend every single available day I had together. I didn't have a car, so I would ride with him to the office, spend the day with him, observe his appointments, listen to seasoned vets at the office making calls, and just learn as much as I could. I wasn't making hardly any money at all, but I didn't care. For me, it was like I had been admitted to the best schooling opportunity I could find. I was learning business, leadership skills, sales skills, communication skills, the list goes on. And I didn't have to pay 20 grand in tuition for it!

I believe this is the missing link for so many young entrepreneurs—the desire to learn. The awareness of the time it takes to become a pro and master your craft. We live in a time where the media is constantly parading example after example of someone who seems to have made it with little to no effort and in no time at all. I was not interested in getting rich quickly, and I was well aware of the sacrifices and discipline it would take for me to have the success I desired. I can close my eyes and remember exactly where I was and how I felt when I decided to take on this entrepreneurship journey full time.

I had been learning everything I could from my dad for about two years. I was now 21, still in college, and about to make a shift in my nursing education, where I would start a new program at a new school in an attempt to get licensed faster and start my nursing career sooner. I had just been admitted into the program with excellent scores and was a few weeks away from starting, but something didn't feel right. I wasn't excited at all. I was dreading it. I knew the path I was on wasn't in alignment with what I wanted for my life. Not only that but here I was looking forward to each chance I got to go to the office with my dad and work in the field, and it felt like this nursing thing was just in my way. I couldn't take it anymore.

I knocked on my dad's office door and said, "Do you have a few minutes? We need to talk; it's important."

"Of course," he said, "come in."

I proceeded to tell him how I was feeling and didn't hold back. "I'm ready to make a move. I know in my heart this is where I am supposed to be. I'm leaving the nursing program and never going back. I don't expect you to understand or even agree, but I just want you to know this is what I have decided and hope that you will provide some wisdom as to what I should do next."

He said, "Here is what I can tell you. You are going to have to work a lot harder than you think. You will face more rejection, more setbacks, more heartbreak and disappointment than you think. When your friends are partying on the weekends, you will be working. When your friends finish school soon and get good jobs, you may still be building your business and not even making half the money they make. I love you and believe you have what it takes. Just know that most people cannot be focused enough, disciplined enough, or mentally tough enough for long enough to win big in anything. But you have the power to be different from most people. And if you can stay disciplined for long enough, it will all be worth it beyond your wildest dreams."

I still remember how I felt. If he was trying to scare me out of my decision, he failed. It had the complete opposite effect! All I wanted to know was that he believed in me and that the hard work would be worth it. I knew mental fortitude and discipline could be developed. I knew I was going to have to grow into an entirely different person to be successful, and that didn't worry me; it excited me. From that day forward, I didn't look back. I was going to make this work or die trying.

They say when you make a big scary decision, adversity comes tumbling down the hill to see what you're made of. Boy is that the truth. It was obvious that I was going to have to build a pipeline of consistent prospects to continue having places to go and people to see. I started by reaching out to the few clients I had helped in my first two years working part-time and asking them for referrals. Although they were happy with how I was able to help them, I had put no real effort at all into cultivating a relationship with them, beyond the transaction, over the past two years. So when I called asking for referrals, I was met with a lot of hesitation and polite rejection, and some had even completely forgotten who I was! Lesson number 1: Understand what business you're in. If it's the *people* business, you won't get anywhere sustainable by treating people like transactions. Relationships aren't pretty important, they're everything. This is a lesson that would take me entirely too long to learn, but a critical one nonetheless.

Realizing this method wasn't getting me anywhere, I decided to change my strategy. I heard in an audio by one of the top leaders in our industry that it was important to make connections with other business owners and entrepreneurs, where we could pass referrals to one another and the relationship would be mutually beneficial. After some more coaching from my dad, I decided I would dedicate the first three hours of each work day (from 9:00 am–12:00 pm) to meeting business owners. I would drive to plazas where I knew a lot of mom-and-pop small businesses were, and I would walk from business to business, asking to speak to the owner. I intended to meet people, set up coffee appointments, and see where that relationship would go! It was a solid plan. Did it work? Initially, no. I was hungry and motivated, but my presentation sucked. I didn't speak with the same confidence I have today. And I was flat-out rejected, left and right. Here I was, several months now into my entrepreneurship journey, and to put it bluntly, I was sucking wind. But I knew I was working hard and getting better. With each failed day, I would meet with my dad and tell him what happened. "Here's what they said and here's what I said." He would correct me and tell me what to say next time.

Entrepreneurship requires the ability to learn by doing. Nobody wants to look bad or feel bad about themselves, so we avoid doing things that we are not good at. There's just no way to become good at anything without first being bad. It's unavoidable. Although I felt defeated with each day of no results, I found refuge in the fact that I was working and learning. I wasn't sitting still! And in due time, as with everything else in life, with enough practice I was going to master this. So I continued with this strategy for some time and met some great people! Most importantly, I developed a thick skin. I became desensitized to the word, "no." Nobody likes rejection, and

I was learning to reframe my perspective on rejection. I found that with each no I got more and more people saying yes and eventually became pretty darn good at talking to people.

I'm grateful for this stage of my career. This was the stage where I learned to create results. Many successful entrepreneurs have a habit of showcasing their wins, their results, and their outcomes and do it so well that it looks easy. People are then enticed by the freedom and lifestyle so much so that they say to themselves, "Hey, that doesn't look so hard. I could do that!"

So you want to quit your job, leave school, and work full time on your business? How are you planning to use your 24 hours? How are you planning to create income versus earning income for the hours you just showed up? I enjoy discussing the losses and the creative process because I know that without it, there would be no glorious outcome! This stage of my career taught me that if I could just learn how to create results, I'd never have to work for somebody in my life. I could transfer that knowledge to any business or industry I'd ever decide to get involved in. So that's what I did. I listened to every audio I could find on prospecting, marketing, networking, and building relationships and applied what I listened to. I tried, I failed, I learned, I pivoted, and in due time, found some of the *right* people. The kind of people who would not only become fabulous clients but would later become great friends and great connectors. We are all one great connection away from an explosion in our business! Never stop connecting, meeting new people, and getting out of your comfort zone.

After years of a relentless pursuit of mastery and a growth mindset, today I can proudly say I have been able to serve families, businesses, and individuals all over the United States. I have had the great fortune to speak for thousands of people on topics like women's empowerment, financial wellness, leadership, and entrepreneurship. While I am incredibly proud of my accomplishments, I am humbly aware of how much life I have left to live and how much impact I have yet to achieve.

My greatest joy is the ability to impact another person's life. I consider it my calling. Over the past decade, I have been able to mentor and coach hundreds of individuals in our industry. These are people who are hungry to change their lives like I was at 19 years old. Nothing excites me more in my business than the opportunity to help equip a motivated person to win, despite all of their faults and shortcomings, and see their vision through to fruition. I believe we have one life to live, and I intend to make the absolute most of it by serving others and making the biggest impact I can for generations to come. In the words of Jackie Robinson, "A life is not important except in the impact it has on other lives."

What is the "why" behind what you do?

On the days when I don't feel like it or when I have suffered temporary losses and doubted myself or considered throwing in the towel, there are a few things that have kept me going. First and foremost, my family. I have been blessed with two amazing children and an incredible husband. I have observed that children do as we do, not as we say. I consider it my duty as their parent to provide an example of what hard work, generosity, leadership, and tenacity look like. As I mentioned in my story, everything I learned about mental toughness in business, I learned from watching my parents. I look forward to the day my children can say the same about me.

I am also moved by the overwhelming need for financial literacy in our communities. In a time where we have more information than we could have ever imagined right at our fingertips, I believe people are more lost and confused than ever before. How do we know what information is credible and in our best interest? Even if the information I got from someone's TikTok video was useful, how do I know where or how to implement it? These are some of the questions I can answer. It is my honor to be able to educate and empower individuals to be able to build financial independence for themselves and their families. I have long subscribed to the belief that if information was given to me to dramatically improve my life, who am I to keep it to myself?

What life or business lessons have created the most growth for you?

When I was 28 years old, my high school sweetheart and I decided to get married. We were madly in love but truthfully, didn't know each other as well as we thought. We had both spent most of our 20s on the grind, building our businesses, and living separately. Much of our relationship was long distance. We had this brilliant plan that we would get married and spend at least a year getting to know each other all over again before having kids. God had a different plan! I gave birth to a beautiful baby girl, exactly nine months after we said, "I do." Here I was, celebrating ten years of entrepreneurship and also entering into a new chapter of my life that had me completely reinventing myself, and it was terrifying. Many women come into motherhood so gracefully. It's as if they were born to do this! They don't seem to skip a beat. To put it mildly, I was not one of those women.

Navigating my new life as a wife, mother, and businesswoman was one of the greatest challenges of my personal and professional life. It is a continuous process of growth and progression that I believe many female entrepreneurs like me face daily. The greatest lesson I learned from this challenge is that we, as women, have the power and, dare I say, responsibility to honor both our families and ambitions simultaneously. The two are not mutually exclusive, as the world would like us to believe. I am constantly reminded that as I chase my dreams, I teach my children the importance of chasing theirs.

I also learned that this idea of making sure you always have a balanced life is misleading, and frankly, dangerous to young ambitious women, starting a family. Balance, to me, is not defined as the facets of my life being separate entities that I should focus on individually and give equal time to. I define it by knowing that the things I prioritize are all a part of my life and interwoven, like a quilt. Ultimately, we must define what matters most to us and give those things the time they require in the season of life that requires it. This may look entirely different for me than it does for you, and that is okay.

What is your ultimate impact?

The skills and knowledge I have developed for over a decade, I use to, first and foremost, educate. We know that all businesses exist to solve a problem. Sometimes, the solution to said problem is simple and doesn't require much to be implemented. If the solution to the money problem families have was simple, it would have been solved a long time ago. What do I mean by "the money problem"? I mean that money touches every area of our lives. It is what most people think about all day long (for better or for worse), and yet, most people don't have a handle on it. I don't mean to say that everyone is broke. I am suggesting that statistically, the majority of people we know do not have a clear, specific plan in place to attain true wealth. The industry would have you believe that the problem can be solved with a new fancy product. I don't believe this to be true.

The core issue lies in a lack of financial literacy. With a better understanding of money basics, individuals can confidently make informed decisions about their finances and product choices. This is akin to a doctor preferring to bill for a service that could be taught for self-care at home, or learning about nutrition before opting for a weight loss pill. Education holds power, and I have the ability to teach something vital for our communities—building, preserving, and safeguarding financial independence. My ultimate impact on the world is to build an army of like-minded, heart-centered professionals to spread this message.

What advice would you give to someone considering entrepreneurship?

Start your journey with an abundance mindset. In Corporate America, workers are often conditioned to believe in limited earning potential and achievement. Drawing from daily experiences with families, guiding them through financial understanding, and outlining steps for their desired financial destination, I can attest that people need a means to overcome these mental hurdles and financial constraints. Entrepreneurship can serve as that means, but aspiring to be an entrepreneur and desiring freedom in life, income, and impact is just the beginning. To succeed in this new chapter, get specific about your goals. Think big: How large do you want your business to be? What does success look like? Define your income goals and envision your ideal retirement. Formulate quality questions as they shape your life. Take your time and think big. You deserve it!

How can people connect with you?

I can be found at www.theamilcarway.com and on Instagram @theamilcarway

I REALIZED THAT TRUE SUCCESS IS NOT JUST MEASURED BY PERSONAL ACHIEVEMENTS, BUT BY THE POSITIVE IMPACT WE HAVE ON OTHERS.

Kathy Binner

CHAPTER 4

IMPACTING YOUR WORLD BY KATHY BINNER

Let me take you back to my childhood, a time when I roamed the sprawling fields of my grandparents' family dairy farm, basking in the sweet scent of hay and the gentle hum of cows. It was a magical place, where hard work and nature's beauty intertwined to shape my upbringing.

From a young age, I was immersed in the rhythms of farm life. Mornings began with the chorus of cows waiting patiently for their milking, their warm breath mixing with the misty air. I would rise extremely early in the morning, rubbing the sleep from my eyes, walk across the field from my house to my grandparents', and join my uncle in the barn. The familiar routine of milking, feeding, and tending to the animals became ingrained in my very being.

But amidst the daily farm work, there was a dream that stirred within me—an unyielding passion for horses. These majestic creatures enchanted me, their grace and power captivating my heart. As I watched them gallop across the fields neighboring our farm, a fire ignited within me, urging me to find a way to make them a part of my life.

My parents and my uncle, with their unwavering support and belief in my dreams, understood the significance of nurturing my aspirations. They recognized that horses would be more than just a hobby for me—they would become my source of solace and a channel for personal growth.

And so, they did something remarkable. With the same determination they brought to the dairy farm, they cleared a portion of the barn, transforming it into a stable, and then added an arena for me to pursue my love for horses.

I vividly remember the first day I stepped into that stable, the scent of fresh hay mingling with the earthy aroma of the horses. My heart soared with anticipation as I groomed and cared for my beloved equine companions. Each moment spent in their presence felt like a sacred connection, a symbiotic bond that transcended words.

As I grew older, my passion for horses intertwined with another endeavor that would shape my teenage years—showing them. The thrill of competition, the meticulous grooming, the camaraderie with fellow equestrians, these experiences became the highlights of my adolescent life.

Preparing for horse shows was no small feat. Countless hours were spent training, perfecting our routines, and honing our skills as a team. The early mornings, the sweat-soaked days under the sun, and the late nights spent in the stable were all fueled by an unquenchable desire to excel.

The ribbons and accolades I earned were not just symbols of victory; they were reminders of the countless hours of hard work, the sacrifices, and the unwavering dedication that brought me to that very moment. But more than the external rewards, the true value lay in the personal growth and resilience I gained along the way.

Growing up on a dairy farm and showing horses as a teenager instilled in me a profound appreciation for the beauty of nature, the value of hard work, and the significance of pursuing one's passions. It taught me the importance of nurturing the dreams of those around us, as my parents and uncle did for me.

But then an encounter with wisdom changed my perspective. I remember listening to a motivational speaker, Brian Tracy, who shared an example that resonated deeply with me. He talked about a horse race, where the winner receives ten times the prize money of the second-place horse, even though the margin of victory is so tiny. It made me reflect.

It's amazing how a small difference, like a few inches or a mere five feet, can determine whether someone is declared a winner or a loser. In the business landscape, it's reminiscent of scenarios like Apple's introduction of the iPhone, where they achieved a remarkable tenfold increase in sales, even with a seemingly modest margin of innovation over other smartphone companies. It makes you think about how we perceive success and failure.

John Maxwell, author and leadership coach, hit the nail on the head when he said that winning and losing are two sides of the same coin. We often fall into the trap of comparing ourselves to others and defining our worth based on those comparisons. We see someone who excels in a particular area and immediately think, "I could never do that. I'm a loser." We don't consider the effort, coaching, and failures they've experienced along the way. Maybe they have dedicated themselves to their goals and dreams, putting in countless hours of hard work. It's nonsensical to compare ourselves to their results and conclude that we're losers because we can't do what they can.

But it's not just about comparing ourselves to others. We also make the mistake of looking at someone else's results and labeling them as losers because they can't do what we can. We forget that everyone has their unique journey and potential. There is no race between us and them; it's always about where we are now and where we can be if we put in the effort. Our focus should be on our growth and reaching our potential.

And the good news is that we all have practically unlimited potential within us. We have the power to choose our direction and keep progressing. As long as we continue moving forward, even if it's just a tiny bit better than yesterday, we will eventually reach our goals. The key is to take those small steps daily, pushing ourselves to do more than before. It's not a matter of whether we can do it; we absolutely can. It's a matter of whether we want to and are willing to put in the effort.

You've already achieved remarkable things in your life—walking, talking, writing—just to name a few. The next step you need to take is small compared to those accomplishments. Your dream is simply a series of those tiny next steps. You have incredible potential within you, but it's up to you to claim it.

From a very young age, I lived with an unyielding desire to make a difference in the world. I yearned to address the pressing social and environmental challenges that plagued our community and beyond. I wanted to make an impact! But everyday life can get in the way.

I was a single mom, barely making ends meet with my two minimum-wage jobs. Every month was a struggle, and I had no health insurance to cover any emergencies that might arise. It felt like I was living on a financial tightrope, with no safety net for my daughter and me. Then something happened that changed my life forever. Memories of that pivotal moment flood my mind and still bring a feeling of hope and fear.

My mom, bless her heart, sat me down one evening. Tears welled up in her eyes as she gently urged me to get on with it. She knew I deserved more, that we deserved more. And that conversation sparked something within me.

I recall that was the turning point that altered the course of my life. I met a nail technician during that challenging time. This incredible young woman made more money in a week than I made in an entire month at my corporate job. It was like a flickering light in the darkness, a glimpse of what was possible. I made a decision. I enrolled in nail school even though it meant sacrificing what little spare time I had left. I was determined to become a part-time nail tech, believing it would give me the financial boost I desperately needed.

I recall the struggles that followed. But the problem was, I was working full time in my corporate job and squeezing in nail appointments whenever I could. The demands of my dual roles left me with no time for my daughter, for the things that truly mattered.

Just when I thought things couldn't get any worse, the nail salon I had joined unexpectedly closed its doors. It felt like a punch to the gut, another blow to my already precarious situation. I took a deep breath with a mix of frustration and determination. And to top it all off, the corporate company I worked for changed. Suddenly, a bachelor's degree became a mandatory requirement. I felt trapped, caught in a never-ending cycle of responsibilities and limitations.

I was overwhelmed with panic. How would I support my daughter and myself without these jobs? Desperation led me to research local colleges, searching for a way to fast-track my bachelor's degree. Simultaneously, I frantically visited countless nail salons, hoping to find a new place to work.

But that's when I truly hit rock bottom. I arrived at the salon one day, filled with anticipation, only to discover it was shuttered, locked behind a For Sale sign. The dream I had clung to vanished right before my eyes.

The following day, I returned to my corporate job, and my boss demanded even more hours. The new owners were relentless in their pursuit of profit, disregarding the toll it took on me physically and emotionally. Tears welled up in my eyes as I reached my breaking point. I was exhausted, running on fumes. It felt like the world was conspiring against me, pushing me further down. In the depths of despair, a flicker of determination ignited within me.

That's when I decided that going full time as a nail tech could provide a better income than my corporate job. It was a risk, but I had to take it for the sake of my daughter and myself.

With my income from being a nail tech, I bought my very own home—a condo. It was a monumental achievement, a symbol of my resilience and determination. And for the first time, I could afford health insurance, offering a glimmer of security for our future.

Then, something happened that changed everything. I discovered a salon where independent contractors paid rent to the owners. A light bulb went off in my mind. Why couldn't I buy my building and rent it out to other nail techs and hair stylists? In 20 years, their rent payments could secure my retirement.

Despite my fears, I leaped and sought a commercial loan to purchase my very own salon building. I immersed myself in learning everything I could about the industry, determined to make this endeavor a success. I made it a priority to make two additional mortgage payments each year, pushing myself to pay off the building ahead of schedule. It was a testament to my unwavering dedication and the desire to create a better future for myself and my daughter.

One day, I looked up and realized all that I had achieved. I saw the possibilities unfolding before me. I could now purchase four more salon buildings, expanding my reach and empowering even more stylists and nail techs. And in a beautiful twist of fate, I started investing in single-family rentals, securing my passive income and ensuring a comfortable retirement.

I now had a passive income and the freedom to live the life I always dreamed of. I could work fewer hours and have the precious opportunity to homeschool my daughter for her final high school years. It was a gift, a chance to bond and guide her as she grew into an incredible young woman.

I now saw myself as a force to be reckoned with—someone in control of her destiny, confident in her abilities, and a provider who could give her daughter the life she deserved. I was not just a business owner; I received the prestigious Chamber of Commerce Business of the Year Award. As if that wasn't enough, I was honored with the Chamber of Commerce Entrepreneur of the Year Award, further solidifying my future journey as an impact entrepreneur, even though I had not stumbled upon that concept yet.

Recalling the moments when I dedicated myself to the care and exhibition of horses, a journey marked by highs and lows, epitomizes the resilience within the human spirit and the strength derived from unwavering determination. With newfound financial freedom, I embraced the luxury of time, no longer compelled to navigate the demanding landscape of minimum-wage jobs, allowing me to truly relish and enjoy life. I finally had time to dream!

I am an avid reader, and one sunny morning as I sipped my coffee and gazed out the window, my mind brimming with ideas, it was then that I stumbled upon a term that ignited my curiosity: impact entrepreneur. Intrigued, I delved deeper into its meaning and discovered that it perfectly encapsulated my aspirations.

What is the "why" behind what you do?

With newfound clarity, I set out on a mission to create a better business that would generate profits and positive change. I knew that my venture had to go beyond financial gains and contribute to the greater good. Poverty, inequality, climate change, access to education and healthcare—these were the pressing issues I aimed to confront—are the "why" behind what I do.

As I embarked on my entrepreneurial journey, I noticed a stark contrast between impact entrepreneurs like myself and my traditional counterparts. While traditional entrepreneurs focus primarily on financial gains, impact entrepreneurs hold a steadfast commitment to making a difference. We believe that business can be a powerful force for social change, and we are determined to prove it.

Meticulously, I designed my business model to provide innovative solutions that addressed the challenges at hand in a sustainable and scalable manner. I sought to create products and services that not only met market demands but also had a positive impact on society and the environment.

Adopting a triple bottom-line approach, I embraced the idea of balancing financial performance with social and environmental outcomes. I understood that measuring success went beyond counting dollars; it involved assessing the positive changes my business brought about in society and the environment. Profit was not the sole indicator of accomplishment; it was the impact I made that truly defined my journey.

As I navigated the intricate world of impact entrepreneurship, I faced numerous challenges and obstacles. But my unwavering dedication and sense of purpose kept me moving forward. I was driven not only by the desire for personal success but also by the deep-rooted belief that my efforts could contribute to a better world.

Along my path, I encountered like-minded individuals who shared my vision and joined forces to amplify our impact. Together, we formed a community of impact entrepreneurs who supported and inspired one another to reach new heights. Our collective efforts created a ripple effect, spreading positive change far and wide.

My entrepreneurial journey was not just about building a successful business; it was about building a legacy of positive social and environmental change. Through my unwavering commitment, I became a beacon of inspiration for others who aspired to combine their entrepreneurial skills and mindset with a burning passion for creating a better world.

With this newfound conviction, I dedicated myself to the mission of giving back, of using my resources and skills to build a legacy of positive social and environmental change. I firmly believed that by doing so, I could contribute to a better future for generations to come.

I started by seeking out organizations and causes that aligned with my values and passion for making a difference. Whether it was promoting education in underserved communities, advocating for environmental sustainability, or championing social justice, I threw myself into the work wholeheartedly.

What role do collaboration and community have in your business?

Recognizing that I couldn't do it alone, I assembled a team of like-minded individuals who shared my vision. Together, we formed a tight-knit community of changemakers, collaborating and supporting each other to amplify our impact. We combined our diverse backgrounds, skills, and expertise, leveraging them to tackle social and environmental challenges head-on.

We began by creating educational programs that empowered individuals from marginalized backgrounds, providing them with the tools and opportunities to thrive. Through scholarships, mentorship programs, and community initiatives, we aimed to break down barriers and unlock the potential of every person, regardless of their circumstances.

Simultaneously, we turned our attention to the environment, recognizing the urgent need for sustainability and conservation. We supported initiatives to promote renewable energy, reduce waste and pollution, and protect fragile ecosystems. By raising awareness and implementing practical solutions, we aimed to preserve our planet for future generations.

Ever since I embarked on my journey of financial freedom and personal growth, I've been driven by a burning desire to empower others with the knowledge and tools to create their passive income streams. I firmly believe that by equipping individuals with the skills and mindset necessary to generate wealth, I could make a meaningful impact on their lives and the world at large.

Driven by this vision, I set out to establish the Kathy Binner International Academy, which would serve as a beacon of knowledge and opportunity for aspiring entrepreneurs from all corners of the globe. I poured my heart and soul into creating a comprehensive curriculum, filled with practical insights, strategies, and step-by-step guidance on being healthy and building passive income businesses.

When asked what surprised him about humanity the most, the Dalai Lama replied,

"Man. Because he sacrifices his health to make money. Then he sacrifices money to recuperate his health. And then he is so anxious about the future that he does not enjoy the present; the result being that he does not live in the present or the future; he lives as if he is never going to die, and then dies having never really lived."

The Kathy Binner International Academy became a thriving community of like-minded individuals eager to learn about better health and passionate about financial independence. We provided not only high-quality educational content but also a supportive network of mentors and fellow students, fostering an environment of collaboration and growth.

As the Kathy Binner International Academy flourished, I made a conscious decision to give back to those less fortunate. I realized that true success is not just measured by personal achievements, but by the positive impact we have on others. With that in mind, I pledged to donate a significant portion of the academy's membership program profits to support charitable causes around the world.

Through careful research and partnerships with reputable organizations endorsed by B1G1 (Business for Good), we identified projects that aligned with our mission of creating a better world. We directed the funds through B1G1 toward initiatives that provided necessities, such as food, clean water, and healthcare to disadvantaged communities. We also invested in long-term sustainable development programs that aimed to uplift entire communities, breaking the cycle of poverty and fostering economic growth.

What life or business lessons have created the most growth for you?

Witnessing the transformative power of our contributions, I knew there was more we could do. Learning that giving back is my greatest joy is the biggest lesson that has created the most growth for me. It pained me to see bright and talented individuals unable to access quality education due to financial constraints. Determined to bridge this gap, I launched the Stephanie Mila Jenkins Initiative educational scholarship program specifically targeting those less fortunate.

The Stephanie Mila Jenkins Initiative scholarship program is designed to provide deserving individuals with the opportunity to pursue their educational aspirations, irrespective of their financial circumstances. We offer financial assistance, mentorship, and resources to help them unlock their full potential and create a brighter future for themselves and their communities.

Through this program, we seek to empower individuals with the knowledge and skills needed to overcome adversity and achieve their dreams. We believe that education is not just a privilege but a fundamental right, and it is our duty to ensure it reaches those who needed it most.

What is your ultimate impact?

Over time, the impact of our efforts grew exponentially. We witnessed students from disadvantaged backgrounds attending prestigious universities, emerging as field leaders, and contributing to their communities. The ripple effect of their success extended far beyond their journeys, inspiring others to pursue education and break through barriers. Inspiring individuals whom I have never met is my ultimate impact!

As I reflect on the journey that led me to where I am today, I am humbled and grateful for the opportunity to create positive change through the Kathy Binner International Academy, the B1G1 charitable contributions, and the Stephanie Mila Jenkins Initiative educational scholarship program. These endeavors have not only transformed the lives of countless individuals but have also allowed me to fulfill my purpose of making a difference in the world. I even had the opportunity to write the foreword for the book *Our Time to RISE* by Steve Pipe and Paul Dunn, enormous supporters and instrumental in bringing B1G1 to the world.

Looking ahead, I am committed to expanding these initiatives, scaling their impact, and continuing to empower individuals to create their paths toward better health, financial independence, and personal growth. Together, let us build a world where everyone has equal access to opportunities, where generosity, better health, and education prevail and where the cycle of poverty is broken.

And so, impact entrepreneurs like me continue to rise, to embrace our role as catalysts for a brighter future. We prove that business can be a force for good, an engine for social and environmental transformation. With each innovative idea and each scalable solution, we drive our ventures forward, creating a harmonious blend of profitability and purpose.

In this bustling era of dreamers and doers, we impact entrepreneurs set out to leave a profound and lasting mark. We know that by harnessing our entrepreneurial spirit and leveraging the power of business, we have the potential to shape a world where positive change thrives. And with my heart full of determination, I continue to embark on our collective mission — to make the impossible possible and build a future that generations to come will be proud to inherit.

How can people connect with you?

Kathy Binner can be found at www.kathybinner.com and on Instagram @kathybinner.

ONE OF THE MANY LESSONS
I LEARNED EARLY ON IS
THAT YOU CAN ONLY GO
SO FAR ALONE.

Rachel Brissenden

CREATING AN IMPACTFUL LEGACY: ENTREPRENEURSHIP, WEB3, AND DISCOVERING YOUR "WHY" BY RACHEL BRISSENDEN

I dedicate this chapter to my father, Daniel Paul Brissenden, who spent many years writing novels and dreaming of becoming a published author. He passed away before that dream became a reality. This is for you, Dad.

Rooted in Purpose and Passion

Purpose and passion have been at the forefront of my entrepreneurial journey. Making an impact and creating a lasting legacy that positively affects people are at the heart of everything I do. Whether you know it or not, you hold the power to shape a life that leaves a lasting impact, a legacy that resonates long after your physical presence has departed.

In the words of the ancient Athenian, Pericles:

"WHAT YOU LEAVE BEHIND IS NOT WHAT IS ENGRAVED IN STONE MONUMENTS, BUT WHAT IS WOVEN INTO THE LIVES OF OTHERS."

—Pericles

Passing the Torch of Legacy

It is August 2023. I am holding my father's manuscript, weeks after his passing. He never got the chance to print or publish his novels, so when he passed away, I went to a print shop shortly after to get his work printed. He spent years perfecting the craft of writing, and it was his life's dream to become a published author. However, he lost his life at the age of 59 after a long, tumultuous battle with mental health before he was able to accomplish that dream. I now like to think of his novels as a way for his thoughts to live on infinitely, his legacy.

He lived his life in pursuit of knowledge, culture, art, and travel. That was his world. I often think of him as an old soul, an ancient Greek philosopher trapped in the modern world. He spent his days thinking about philosophy, language, the great renaissance artists, and studying the dimensions of ancient Greek and Roman columns that he often realistically drew, painted, and sculpted. He taught me a variety of lessons from a young age which have deepened my appreciation for knowledge, culture, art, and the great innovators throughout history to this day.

My father likely read over a thousand books in his lifetime. Later in life, with all that accumulated knowledge, he discovered an insatiable passion for writing. He wrote multiple novels before passing away. It is now my mission to get his work published and to continue his dream by sharing this story and now becoming a published author myself.

While he spent his life in pursuit of knowledge, he tended to neglect his health and wellness, which ultimately led to an early death. The loss of my father has pushed me to prioritize my health, both mental and physical, even more, understanding that these things are not compartmentalized but very much connected.

So, what does all this have to do with being an impact entrepreneur? Well, it all began with a season of self-discovery and reinvention.

Ikigai as a Vehicle for Self-Discovery: The Lessons That Created the Most Growth for Me

My journey of self-reinvention kicked off during a profound phase of introspection when COVID-19 hit. I started contemplating deeply how I could make a tangible difference in people's lives. Coming from an art school background, I have always felt more creatively inclined. However, with the world in a state of calamity, I found myself grappling with persistent questions, such as the following:

- What drives me, and what is my purpose?
- How can I use my unique gifts and passions to positively impact the world?
- How can I use my creativity to make a tangible difference in people's lives?

During this period of introspection, a few things helped me gain more clarity into my reason for being. Years ago, my father introduced me to the Japanese philosophy *Ikigai*, aimed at helping one discover their purpose. Throughout the years, this often crossed my mind. When the pandemic unfolded, I decided to explore this concept further and began sketching out the Ikigai Venn diagram in pursuit of answers.

After writing this out multiple times, an idea started to pop into my mind—I glanced across the room at a juicer that my mother had bought me for my birthday. For me to really go deeper and find answers, I knew I needed a clear body and mind. So I decided to embark on a juice cleanse, which made me clearer, more focused, and energized each day. I felt so good that I knew this was a gift I wanted to give to others. Getting healthier brought me closer to my life's calling, and I'll walk you through the exercise that guided me there.

Finding Your "Why" Exercise

Step 1: To start out, draw a Venn diagram with four intersecting circles on a sheet of paper. Allow the circles to intersect, creating a central region where all four overlap. This central intersection signifies your Ikigai or the sweet spot where your passion, mission, vocation, and profession align. Use this visual representation to explore and discover the areas in your life that bring fulfillment and purpose.

Step 2: Write the following in the circles:
"What the world needs"
"What I can get paid for"
"What I'm good at"
"What I love"

Step 3: In each circle, under these words, write 3–5 examples in relation to the category.

Note: Take your time to provide thoughtful responses. At the intersection of these answers, somewhere in between, I hope your life's purpose becomes more evident to you! If not, that's okay too. Feel free to come back to this exercise as many times as you'd like and discover the answers in your own time.

Something that continuously came up for me while doing this exercise was what the world needs. At the time, with the collective fear of getting sick from COVID, people wanting to build immunity, all while we're facing a climate crisis, the idea to create something that truly benefits people and the planet became more in focus.

What if I **created** (what I'm good at) a **business** (what I can get paid for) focusing on **helping people** (what I love) and by helping them **prioritize wellness** while **giving back to the planet** (what the world needs) using sustainable business practices?

Piecing this all together led me to start my first business.

Starting my First Business: Elixir of Life

I didn't know it at the time, but the seed for my business, Elixir of Life, had been implanted in my mind, and that seed would grow into a flowering business that would go on to help people and make a tangible difference in people's lives. I knew that I needed to have a deeply reflective moment to decide the name of my business once I identified what I wanted to create. I decided to meditate on the name, with a notebook and a pen in hand. The name appeared to me as if it was already deep within my subconscious:

Elixir of Life. Those were the words I wrote on my page. Nothing more, nothing less. I had the name.

I went on to study holistic nutrition at the Institute for Integrative Nutrition (IIN), create my menu, the logo, branding, and began vending at festivals and working with clients individually. Eventually, I also got my products into stores in Southern California, including the plant-based chain Nice Guys!

It made sense to me for the business to be rooted in the theme of alchemy. Alchemists throughout history tried for years to combine elements to create liquid gold, an elixir to sustain life indefinitely and cure illness. I also decided that if I'm creating something good for people's health, I must also create something good for the planet, which is why I ended up using sustainable packaging and working to support various environmental nonprofits such as Stand Up To Trash. Everything is interconnected, and a sick planet will ultimately translate to sicker people. It's all symbiotic.

Elixir of Life being so positively received by clients and customers proved to me that we have the ability to create the life and legacy of our choosing, and it all starts with an idea. A simple exercise to find my life's purpose led me to create a business that helped people. It also taught me that we have a lot of the answers within us. No one told me to start my business. I sat with myself, analyzed my values and my "why," and I delved into entrepreneurship without a handbook. I followed my gut and what I know to be right. I believe that is an essential part of entrepreneurship: being tapped into your inner guide and making decisions that are aligned with your values. Nourishing my body and contemplating my "why" or Ikigai helped me to create something and get tapped into a purpose-driven mission.

The Evolution of My First Business: Lessons Learned

An essential component to emphasize about entrepreneurship is that running a business is *definitely* not a walk in the park! It takes so much more work than you could even imagine when you first get started. It really is like having a baby, and that baby is yours to nurture and grow.

One of the many lessons I learned early on is that you can only go so far alone. I did much of the early days of my business on my own, creating the cleansing packages, cutting, peeling, juicing, driving to drop off deliveries, and stocking shelves at stores. Nothing was easy, and nothing was handed to me. I was the graphic designer, the product designer, the business developer, the social media manager, the delivery driver, and the juicer! As a founder, I quickly learned that you initially wear all of the hats until it's time to scale the business.

It took me the better part of a year to realize that it was okay to ask for help. In fact, it's essential if you want to run a successful business that truly makes an impact. So I began hiring trusted individuals to vend with me at events and even create a website for my business. I am eternally grateful to Omzee Pitchford and Eureka Marie Brown for the times they supported me and completely saved me, caring for my business with the same level of passion and dedication that I did.

Below, I've provided some insight from Eureka, who formerly worked with me on Elixir of Life. She illustrates through her words just how impactful the power of collaboration can be:

"The first time I saw Rachel, I was inspired. She was vending at a festival in San Diego, I believe. Her dedication, her style, her logo, her idea, they all fit so perfectly. At the wellness retreat where she vended, her juices gave people life. Hence the name Elixir of Life!

"I've always been searching to be a part of something meaningful. So when she asked me to come help with vending at an upcoming festival, I was honored! That's when I got to

see firsthand the dedication it takes to actually pull it off. From running around trying to find generators for power, to setting up, to tearing down. It was both a lot of work and a blessing. Seeing the joy on people's faces brought me life. Getting to connect with people in a meaningful way reminded me of just how precious life can be.

"Now, looking back on it years later, I can finally say that I found inspiration for my own life from the work I did with Rachel. She has been an inspiration for me to create meaningful change and impact in the world!"

—Eureka Marie Brown

My entrepreneurial journey started here. I then discovered a new way of working that would completely transform everything, where I could apply the skills I've learned. This was something that I didn't foresee coming, and it went on to change the landscape of everything I've built.

My Ultimate Impact and the Discovery of DAOs and Web3

As my entrepreneurial journey started to take flight, a friend mentioned a term to me. Three letters that completely changed my life: DAO (decentralized autonomous organizations). Initially, I had no idea what they were talking about. Things like crypto and DAOs were all a mystery to me initially; however, I was intrigued and hungry to learn more! I got invited into calls and had the chance to get introduced to the space.

While I didn't understand what these individuals were talking about yet, I had a feeling deep down in my gut that they were going to change the world for the better somehow. They spoke with such passion and determination to implement solutions to not only improve a broken financial system but create a new one.

As my days concluded, after working and running my business, I found myself more and more eager to jump in on calls, chats, and Twitter spaces to learn as much as I could about DAOs.

Before I explain what a DAO is (hang tight!), I'll explain some fundamental systemic challenges we are facing. This will hopefully help to illustrate why they exist.

Prevalent systemic issues include the disproportionate control exerted by big banks and corporations, a widening wealth gap, and the erosion of job satisfaction, as highlighted by the Gallup State of the American Workplace Study, where 69 percent of American workers were found to be disengaged. These issues extend beyond the United States, and I feel confident in doing the work to combat these issues. Below, I've included a quote from the vice mayor of Berkeley, reflecting on ongoing efforts to tackle problems:

"Recognizing the challenges our world faces, Rachel actively seeks ways to help where solutions can be implemented and does not hesitate to jump in where she can make a difference.

"Since our initial meeting, she has now become a dedicated supporter of my efforts to bring about positive change in the Berkeley community and beyond. I have no doubt that she will keep going and continue making an impact."

—Ben Bartlett, Vice Mayor of Berkeley

Emerging as part of the solution to tackling systemic issues, a global collective movement has begun, all stemming from the novel Bitcoin white paper published by the anonymous individual (or group of individuals) named Satoshi Nakamoto. Many refer to this as Web3, and it encompasses the creation of blockchain technology, cryptocurrencies, and the evolution of the internet toward digital ownership. All of these have contributed to the formation of DAOs.

What's a DAO?

This is a question I've been thinking about for some time. I've become increasingly fascinated by the idea as I delved deeper into the world of working in Web3. The term "DAO" stands for decentralized autonomous organization, which is a new organizational structure that has come along with the rise of blockchain and cryptocurrencies, being very aligned in their ideologies. DAOs are member-owned organizations without a central authority or leadership. According to Consenys.net, "It is essentially a community-led entity with no central governing body, built on a blockchain using smart contracts."

My first career opportunity in the Web3 space was entirely focused on DAOs, specifically DAO tooling. I began this new career journey at ETHDenver, where I publicly spoke and embarked on my path into the industry. My initial role focused on facilitating DAO operations for a large blockchain protocol, where I was given an opportunity to start my career by one of my earlier mentors, Samuel P. Harrison. Sam would say that DAOs share the following essential components:

- Shared interest
- Shared asset
- Shared responsibility

I admire DAOs for these very reasons and because they allow for members to show up and work autonomously on something they are passionate about collectively, with no CEO or boss. Everyone shows up as equals to make decisions autonomously, distributing funds when needed through democratic voting processes. Now you may be thinking, "Wait! Rachel, are you saying there's a way to run a business without entrusting funds to big centralized banks, and there's no boss?" Yes, that's correct! A new, more equitable way to run businesses has emerged, and we're all just beginning to see the possibilities.

A Pivot to Self-Sovereign Work and Making a Global Difference

One of the complications associated with DAOs, blockchain, and cryptocurrency is that at present, they're not easily integrated into well-established systems. Earning in decentralized currency doesn't come with a W2, which can make things like tax reporting and compliance more complicated. Fortunately, as I continued working in the industry, I discovered a project, Opolis, that offered a way to pay myself payroll while gaining access to benefits I would get at a corporate position, all while being in business for myself.

Leading partnerships at Opolis connected me to numerous DAOs and Web3 groups, aiding hundreds in embracing self-employment, including myself. Members are now able to do the work that they love, while having the freedom and flexibility to work from anywhere, with anybody, and as much as they please. More importantly, members have the sovereignty to own their work instead of the other way around, while having the confidence of doing so with proper compliance and access to benefits!

My Web3 career has led me to opportunities of my dreams. I eventually began hosting and producing the Crypto Sapiens podcast, where I cultivated a deep passion for educating on blockchain and related topics. Through the podcast and Twitter spaces I've hosted over the years, I've interviewed over two hundred industry thought leaders and projects. All of this truly sparked my interest in public speaking, leading me to global travel and facilitating workshops at UCLA and USC. I've since become involved with the University of Ethereum, collaborating with universities and blockchain clubs worldwide to advance blockchain education. This path has extended to consulting on a political campaign, collaborating with the vice mayor of Berkeley, and aiding the princess of the Mende Royal family of Sierra Leone in fundraising efforts through the blockchain space for improved access to clean drinking water in her country.

"Years ago, I met Rachel during the Web3 Ethereum event, ETHDenver. Since we've connected, Rachel has invited me to work with the University of Ethereum, where she curates weekly educational workshops for students, universities, and blockchain clubs around the world.

"For our workshop, she brought in the Vice Mayor of Berkeley, Ben Bartlett, to discuss how blockchain bonds can be leveraged as a solution to fund increased access to clean drinking water for communities in Sierra Leone.

"Since that discussion, Rachel has taken proactive steps to support our mission at Sierra Leone Rising. She is currently working on fundraising efforts to kick-start the construction of a well in the village of Bumpe! Outside of this, her focus has been primarily on how she can solve real world problems with blockchain and make a tangible and positive impact.

"I appreciate Rachel's dynamic spirit and her commitment to supporting people around the world!"

—*Princess Sarah Culberson of Sierra Leone*

Moving Forward to Craft Your Ultimate Impactful Legacy

In conclusion, if you wish to go far, go together. Through my journey, I have merged my values, passion for creativity and wellness, and the transformative power of Web3, all the while emphasizing the magic of collaborative efforts in the decentralized space. My ultimate goal is to make an impact on the world by creating a tangible positive difference in people's lives through holistic wellness, empowering people to be financially empowered, and having sovereignty over their livelihoods.

Now, circling back to the exercise in this chapter, I challenge you to find the most compelling life purpose you can, with respect to the answers you've found. My hope for you is that taking the time to identify what you love, what the world needs, what you can get paid for, and what you're good at has the power to help you forge an impactful path and meaningful legacy! Hopefully writing all this down physically, will guide you toward envisioning these things for yourself.

Finally, here's a bonus question for you! What is the ultimate impact that you would like to leave on the world? Take a few moments to reflect on this. Really think about how you envision yourself making an impact on the world and leaving a lasting legacy. What does this look like for you? I hope that answering the questions and envisioning this brings you closer to a deeper understanding of your life's purpose.

I began this chapter with a discussion of my father's dream to be a novelist, a dream that sadly went unfulfilled during his lifetime. It thrills me to think that through tools like Web3, DAOs, and holistic wellness, we can empower an entire generation of humans to discover not only their "why" but achieve it in ways never before imagined. In that way, my father's legacy—his pursuit of knowledge, culture, art, and innovation—lives on. I hope that this chapter has helped you to tap into your "why" and has inspired you to go out and create an impactful legacy that will continue to serve the greater good, long after your physical presence has departed.

How can people connect with you?

I can be found at https://linktr.ee/rachelroseb and on LinkedIn @Rachel Brissenden.

IF YOU CHOOSE TO SEE OPPORTUNITIES ALL AROUND YOU, YOU WILL FIND THEM.

Dr. Rocco Crapis

CHAPTER 6

MAKING PROBLEMS INTO OPPORTUNITIES BY DR. ROCCO CRAPIS

Some people are born entrepreneurs.

Me? Not so much.

The fact is most people who knew me in my younger years probably wouldn't have pegged me as the entrepreneur type. Today, I'm a chiropractor by trade, but that wasn't always the plan. You see, I come from a small town and grew up in a very working-class community. In school, I did about as much work as I needed to do in order to stay academically eligible to play football, no more and no less.

Don't get me wrong, I was a hard worker. I always had part-time jobs while I was in high school, and during the summers, it wasn't uncommon for me to work sixty-plus hours a week. I went to college to play football, but that's about all I wanted to do. I really hadn't given much thought to the sort of career I wanted to pursue after I got out. By all accounts, I was on track to lead the life of a salaried employee somewhere or an hourly wage earner, and I was fine with that. That was my mindset on life.

If there's one thing I've learned over the years, it's that mindset is everything. And I can tell you the exact moment when my mindset changed forever.

It happened on a hot summer day. At the time, I was working at a trucking company, where my job was to load and unload freight from tractor trailers. It was long hours of grueling work, and I was good at it. Back then, you got a printed manifest of everything that was on the trailer, along with a bunch of other unimportant information that pertained to the trailer in question that nobody ever really paid attention to. Loaders like me used the manifests to check that everything was accounted for when loading and unloading. We called it "breaking the trailer."

One day, while sitting on the forklift and eating my lunch, I started looking at some of that unimportant information on the manifest that nobody paid attention to. That's when I noticed that down at the bottom of the printout, there was a section that listed how much money the company made off of each trailer.

I remember it vividly. That week, I had gotten a paycheck for eighty-two hours of work, making $15.15 an hour. (And, just to be clear, this was not a two-week paycheck. We normally worked five twelve-hour shifts per week, but I was always picking up extra hours whenever I could.) I had just gotten done breaking a trailer. And because I was good at my job, it had only taken me about one hour to break this trailer.

As I looked at the manifest, I found myself confused. If the numbers I was looking at were right, it meant that in one hour, in the time it had taken me to earn $15.15, I had made the company thousands of dollars.

This just didn't make any sense. I was only a kid at the time, but a lot of my coworkers were grown men with families who had been working there for years doing the same work. Even the top earners in their positions were only making something like $21.00 an hour. The people in charge, the ones who ran the company and signed the paychecks and didn't have to do any of the dirty work like breaking trailers, must have been making hundreds of times more money for an hour of work!

I could have chosen to see this as a problem. (The bosses are screwing me! I don't make enough money!) Instead, subconsciously, I saw it as an opportunity.

Reframing problems as opportunities: The lesson that created the most growth for me

Without realizing it, I was going through a transformation. Sitting on the forklift that day, with the trailer manifest in one hand and my paycheck in the other, I found myself wondering, *If I put eighty-two hours of work a week in for myself, what would happen?* The answer came pretty quickly: *I don't know yet. But it's got to be better than this!* It was then that I realized, "I am *not* doing this for the rest of my life!"

For me, this was a revolutionary concept. Most of the people from my small town were of the mindset that you should get a good, secure job and stay there. That was what life was supposed to be. But the security they enjoyed was an illusion. They would always live at the mercy of the guy signing their paychecks; their work and their potential for success were always going to rest in someone else's hands.

I didn't know what I was going to do as an entrepreneur yet; I doubt I could have even told you what an entrepreneur *was* at that point. But I knew one thing: I wasn't going to be working for somebody else for the rest of my life.

I couldn't have known it at the time, but by making that key mindset shift that day, I was engaging the brain's reticular activating system (RAS). I've heard this part of the brain described as a heat-seeking missile because once it's found its target, it locks on and follows it wherever it goes. It's what led me to move out of my small town, go to chiropractic school, get my doctorate, and open up my own small business to serve my community and help the people around me unleash their innate potential and heal from within.

You see, thoughts are like bullets. Once they exist, they are like a bullet leaving the gun; they can't be taken back. And once they're out there in the ether, they then have the potential to become manifest based on your attention to them.

My RAS, my goal-oriented brain, became engaged in seeking out ways to achieve my mission. And, what do you know! I suddenly started seeing opportunities all over the place that would lead me toward achieving that very goal.

Show me someone with a strong, fortified mindset, and the belief that they can achieve whatever they set out to do, and I'll show you a person who will figure out how as they go, regardless of what knowledge they have.

What is the "why" behind what you do?

Years later, I unexpectedly found myself at the lowest point in my life.

By all appearances, things were going well. I was a happily married man. My wife and I, both chiropractors, were partners in business as well as in life. We had a young daughter, and we were committed to raising her right and building her into the ultimate little badass with purpose.

But, deep down, I was in turmoil. Our practice was struggling. Even worse, *I* was struggling. I felt lost. I didn't know why, but I felt like I was in a deep valley and struggling to come up out of it. This lasted for about nine months. And then, just when I thought it couldn't get any worse, it did. My wife decided she didn't want to be married anymore.

One bitter divorce later, I was suddenly a lone entrepreneur, with shared custody of my child, struggling to keep a business afloat on my own. I was heartbroken. I felt dejected. I had no money. And on top of it all, I now had to learn how to be a single dad to my daughter.

I didn't know what came next for me. Where was I supposed to go from here? What was I supposed to do? At my absolute lowest, I found myself lying on my bathroom floor feeling defeated. I didn't even want to rise up to face this struggle anymore.

This wasn't part of the plan, I thought as I lay there, tears running down my face. *This is NOT how things were supposed to go.*

Fortunately, it's sometimes easier to change for someone else than it is to change for yourself. I realized I had a daughter who was depending on me. And if I was only going to have her for 50 percent of the time, I would have to be locked in and 100 percent focused for that 50 percent. If I was going to be a single dad, I was going to do everything in my power to be the best single dad on Earth. And if I wanted to be the best single dad on Earth, I was going to have to learn how.

But the more I looked around, the more disappointed I was with the resources available to fathers. There really weren't a lot of good places to learn for normal, real dads. I realized that there was an opportunity here. Surely, there were other men like me looking for resources like this. So, why not share my journey of learning with other men? And that's how, in the middle of one of the most painful seasons of my life, *It's Dad Time* was born.

The *It's Dad Time* podcast represents my life's goal to bring my message of deep healing, transformation, and creation to the masses of dads out there. We do this by sharing stories of fathers from all walks of life. This is a place where we share our struggles, successes, and failures, and it has quickly grown from a simple idea to a massive movement.

What life or business lessons have created the most growth for you?

At some point after the divorce, I started to notice that during the weeks when I had my daughter, she was using a certain phrase an awful lot. It was three simple words: *The problem is.*

Personally, I tend to overthink the words that are coming out of my mouth, especially when I'm speaking to my daughter. Words have power, after all. At first, I wasn't sure why those words, "the problem is," bothered me so much. But as time went on, I realized that it was something I'd been hearing my entire life without ever really noticing how negative and detrimental they were.

The masculine brain tends to look at the world and see a series of problems that need to be solved. It's a trait that is deeply coded in our DNA, stretching back through the millennia, and it has empowered men to help them survive in hostile environments, thrive in the midst of difficulties and stress, and protect and provide for their families even at great personal sacrifice. The relative safety and comforts of the modern world that we all take for granted today are due in no small part to the powerful problem-solving capabilities that come innately equipped in the masculine brain.

But this framework doesn't always serve us well. Men are constantly on the lookout for problems that need to be solved. When we find them, we focus our energy on solving them. (Even when there *aren't* any problems, a real man will find one.) And, as an unfortunate extension of this process, fathers tend to see parenting as a series of problems to solve.

These days, I can't stand the word "problem." I feel so strongly about it that my daughter has learned that in my house, we don't even use that word. We substitute it with a different word: opportunity.

This is such a minor switch in vocabulary. And yet, it changes everything. What happens to your brain when you see nothing but problems? For one thing, it puts you on the defensive 100 percent of the time. Your life becomes more about *reacting* to external stimuli than taking action and being proactive.

If you're not convinced, compare the following two thought processes:

1. There are so many problems around me that I can't solve them all.
2. There are so many opportunities around me that I can't even execute on them all.

You tell me, which one of these mindsets is more powerful?

The divorce had left me devastated, heartbroken, and alone. I could have chosen to see my new, unexpected identity as a single father as a problem. That's where most men's minds probably would have gone. But it's amazing how when you refuse to see problems, opportunities start springing up all over the place.

So, how about you? Do you see problems around you? Or do you see opportunities?

I know this difference may seem trivial at first, but if you start a sentence with "the problem is," you then have to follow up by defining and verifying the problem, imbuing it with power. If, on the other hand, you say, "the opportunity is," you don't get the chance to continue down that negative thought process. You cut the problem off at its knees, you reject the victim mentality, and you build mental fortitude. You instantly shift gears away from problems toward solutions. As a result, while others are seeing problems that need to be solved, you are reverse-engineering situations to find the opportunities inherent in literally everything.

I will acknowledge that it can be difficult to make that sort of mental shift. It can feel uncomfortable. You literally have to change the hardwiring of your brain. But once you do it, it starts snowballing. Everything becomes an opportunity. Before long, it can almost feel exhausting. You start to realize, there are a lot of opportunities around me every day.

It's all about mindset

I began this chapter by stating that mindset is everything. And the deeper I get into *It's Dad Time*, the more I find this to be true.

At first glance, the problem-solving masculine brain doesn't seem to be the best fit for raising kids. Perhaps this is why so many of us had fathers who seemed quick to criticize. Instead of seeing the things we were good at, seeing what we were doing right, their problem-solving brains defaulted to focusing on what we were doing wrong—what we needed to *improve* at. If a child is a talented artist but not very good at math, math becomes the focus. If a child can hit a baseball but can't ride a bike, bike riding is probably all his father wants to talk about.

In their own way, dads are just trying to help. It's why you hear so many fathers yelling from the sidelines at kids' sports events. The benches are filled with masculine brains trying to solve the problems they're seeing. "Head up! Feet apart! Swing hard! Hustle!" But children, in the moment, aren't in that problem-solving mindset. They are hearing *criticism*. They are hearing that they aren't good enough. In fact, I'm willing to bet that even as you're reading this, you may be thinking, "Man, I feel like this all the time, even when I win!"

Trust me, you're not alone.

Let me ask you this. What's more important: teaching your son how to throw the perfect spiral or teaching them the mindset that they can do anything they put their mind to, whether that something is throwing a perfect spiral or playing Beethoven on the piano?

Let's be honest with ourselves. Children can always figure out how to do something. They can learn it at any time and from anyone, the same way they learn to read and write from their teachers in school. The map that leads where they want to go—no matter where it is or what they want to achieve—will always be waiting out there in the world for them to discover.

But who's going to teach them the right mindset? It's up to you and you alone to teach your children the mindsets they need to thrive. And it all starts within you.

What is your ultimate impact?

Chiropractic is about eliciting a healing response through a power that is already within you. *It's Dad Time* is a highly focused extension of that. My goal is to give people, including dads, the tools that help them get where they need to be. But I can't help but notice that so much of the work we do on ourselves is about fixing what's wrong, healing what's broken, rebuilding what's been torn down, and rewiring incorrect neural pathways.

As parents, we have the opportunity to make sure that our kids are properly hardwired from the very beginning. Imagine if someone had done that for you! Now, you have the potential to do it for someone else.

My work with *It's Dad Time* is about helping a generation of fathers embrace the fact that they are creators, not merely problem-solvers. That power is already within you. The goal is to awaken fathers to the chance they have to create a new generation of men and women who see opportunities in everything instead of problems and view everything from that perspective.

Here's what I want you to know, Dads…

- If you choose to see problems everywhere, that's exactly what you'll find. And if you choose to see opportunities all around you, you will find them.
- When everything goes wrong, be grateful that you get to show your stuff.
- On a terrible day, when it all seems to come crashing down at once, be grateful that you get to be an example to your child of how to get through tough times.
- And when all you can see are the problems, be grateful for the opportunity to teach your child how a man uses his focus to find solutions.

As an entrepreneur, this is how you build everything. It's why my chiropractic business, which could have easily never recovered from the difficult times I went through, has instead grown exponentially in just a few years. It's why, the other day, when a colleague explained to me that the days of people driving an hour just to visit their chiropractor are long gone, I just sat and smiled, knowing that I have people who drive an hour and a half one way for their appointments with me, people who fly from several states away to see me, and people who fly me across the entire country and to other countries around the world, just to stay under my care. And it's why *It's Dad Time* has grown so quickly.

It's Dad Time is not just interviews with parents or fluff stories meant to inspire or motivate. My goal is to give you the practical tools that you can pull out of your back pocket over and over again to empower and build your child's mind and to change your life and the trajectory of your children's lives.

I can give you all the right tools and the perfect plan, and you still won't get it right the first time. (Trust me, I'm a single dad. I follow recipes all the time, using all the right ingredients and all the right tools, and they still turn out wrong.) Without the right mindset, you'll stop. But you have to keep going. It just takes repetition.

Bottom line: Getting divorced made me a better father. Maybe that wasn't the ideal way things could have happened, but that's my story.

The other day, my daughter was on a rope swing on the playground. It was an obstacle she had never tried before on her own, and she was a little scared.

"What if I fall?" she said.

"It's okay to fall," I told her. "It's also okay to feel some fear. But what do I always say? What do we say to fear?"

She looked at me and smiled. "Not today."

That's what we say to fear. Not today.

Failure is part of the process. You're going to fall down once in a while, but part of learning is figuring out how to keep going in spite of the falls. You can't achieve anything without the mental fortitude to withstand failure and keep going. It's what got me up off that bathroom floor to begin with. That and a little girl was depending on me.

When you fall, get back up. And make sure your kids *see* you get back up. They're watching. And they're learning. Your children aren't problems. Every one of them is the very definition of opportunity.

At its core, life is simple. If you focus on what you're looking for, you will find the breadcrumbs.

Kids want to be loved, seen, and heard. Deep down, that's all any of us want. It's what you want, it's what your clients want, and it's what your patrons want. Meet these three needs and I promise you that 99 percent of your problems go away.

You can do this.

How can people connect with you?

I can be found at www.alchemychiro.com and on Instagram @ alchemy_chiropractic.

I CAN'T THINK OF A BIGGER CHANGE AGENT THAN THE ENTREPRENEURIAL SPIRIT.

Debbie Golden

CHAPTER 7

THE UNQUENCHABLE ENTREPRENEURIAL SPIRIT
BY DEBBIE GOLDEN

My first job was at an ice cream parlor owned by my dad in Wisconsin; I was 12 years old. I would set up the store, make all the food, serve the people, clean the tables, and close up for the night. Basically, I did it all. Even though my dad owned the parlor, he still had to work a steady job as a social worker. But through this experience, my father gifted me with the entrepreneurial spirit.

For the next four years, I helped run all of my dad's side businesses, cultivating that entrepreneurial spirit like a tended garden. But starting at 16, I found myself getting trapped in a box. Instead of running my dad's businesses, I worked for Hardee's because I thought that was what you were supposed to do. I then went to college so that I could find a steady job because I thought that was what you were supposed to do. And that led to me working for someone else in the consumer packaged goods industry because I thought that was what you were supposed to do. I was responsible for building relationships between the manufacturers and retailers. And over the next nine years, I made it possible for many famous brands to become more widely available.

As I climbed the corporate ladder, I gained all the buzzy corporate benefits like the guaranteed salary, company car, bonus structure, and retirement plan. Even though I had all of those things that most people call comfort and security, something was stirring in me. I realized that while I was making $1.5 million in commissions for this company, my own income was capped, based on what *someone else* thought was fair. *Someone else* was determining my value, controlling my destiny. I was no longer building my own dream because I was caught up in *someone else's*. And all of this came with a cost: that entrepreneurial spirit, instilled by my dad, now laid dormant. But little did I know at the time that I was setting myself up for a different kind of success, where all that knowledge and expertise would pivot me somewhere else.

At age 33, the entrepreneurial spirit awoke again. This awakening wasn't a mere itch that I could ignore; it was an inner indisputable piece of action that I knew I had to take. Because I knew that I could do this same kind of work, but on my own, in my own firm. It was time to transition into freedom.

Due to the strong relationships I built with the buyers at major retailers, I was able to discuss my newfound plans with them. Thankfully, they were all in support of me going out on my own and even helped by recommending clients to me.

I am not going to tell you that the path to starting my own firm was easy. I was filled with all of the normal worries and insecurities that come with starting your own business. Will clients want to hire me? Will I make money? How will I pay for healthcare? Will I make enough for retirement? I pushed forward. The first few months of building my firm were extremely hard. I was missing that regular guaranteed income.

Then one day it all just started to click. I started getting more clients through word of mouth and deeper relationship building. As their brands were getting bigger, I was able to help them grow even more. Through the skills I learned in my previous job, I was able to get their products in prominent shelf locations at store level all across the country. I found a great rhythm professionally, personally, and financially. I had a huge house, nice cars, and more time than ever with my three great kids. I made over $600K representing just one client! I was on top of the world; and from the outside, you would have thought I had it all, but I didn't.

In 2017, I got divorced. This caused me to land in a financial hole that I needed to dig myself out of. It set me back so far financially that I found myself not only running my own firm, but also having to take a job in Corporate America again for a large CPG Brand. With two full-time jobs, this was a forced pivot.

As time passed and I started recovering both emotionally and financially, I found myself, once again, feeling that stirring inside of me. But this time, it was a little different because I was now more broke than ever. I was stuck in a vicious cycle of endless virtual calls, travel, hotel rooms, and meetings. I was completely handcuffed by Corporate America to this lifestyle. My teenage boys were almost in college, and my time left with them at home was slipping away. My parents were getting older, and my time with them was also slipping away. The realization that you can't stop time and it is vulnerable and fragile was weighing on me. Even though I sold over $1B in consumer products at this point in my career, it all felt empty now. Because in all that success, I did not fulfill my true passion and calling: to serve others. It was time to pivot again, and I was eager to do so with a greater inner peace than ever before.

One night, I was drinking wine and watching *The Bachelor* in my living room. As I scrolled through my phone on the couch, I stumbled across an ad on Instagram about making money online. The ad's wording about gaining more time and financial freedom made me pause long enough to stop scrolling and click on it. And that was my introduction to affiliate marketing. As an affiliate marketer, you get paid a commission for selling other people's products. What drew me to this was the promise of time flexibility, and that I could make money with just a few hours of my day on the phone.

If I pursued affiliate marketing, I could teach my kids how to do this as well, and that could set them up financially. This was my ticket out of Corporate America, providing me with the time freedom I was in desperate need of, while offsetting the cost of college and retirement. I wanted to give it a try, while still holding on to my two full-time jobs. So I did it, and I failed.

After 25 years of completely knowing the playing field, I was a newbie. Taking the role of a student humbled me because this required more active engagement on social media, and I had a lot to learn. But because of that failure, I was able to grow. Affiliate Marketing ultimately opened the door to a whole new world for me. The whole idea of making money online was a concept completely foreign to me, along with the idea of regularly posting content on social media. This wealth of knowledge served as a launching pad for my next pivot.

I stumbled upon something called digital marketing. I did some pretty extensive research on this, and felt like it had a lot of similarities to my career in consumer packaged goods. The biggest difference is that I would be selling and marketing digital products instead of physical products, but through a similar business process.

Digital products encompass a wide range of goods and services that are delivered and consumed electronically. Examples of digital products include online courses, ebooks, coaching, movies, music, art, NFTs, apps, and so many more. The e-Learning segment is going to be worth $325 Billion by 2025.

Digital marketing is the long-term strategy that moves with the trajectory of the world and how consumers of today are shopping. Because of this, the booming growth of digital marketing is extremely attractive.

I found a digital marketing course called "The Roadmap." As a complete beginner, this felt like everything I needed to get started in this new world. The course was professionally done and had the look and feel of the caliber of professionalism that I was used to from Corporate America. The video modules take someone step-by-step from a beginner level to build everything someone needs to start an online automated business. People do not need to be tech savvy to take this course and implement the lessons.

As I dug deeper into this course and digital marketing, I quickly learned that through the automated systems that I was setting up, it's truly possible to make passive income. Making money while you sleep is something that people looking to make money online dream of. In a very short amount of time I learned about sales funnels, email marketing campaigns, and how to create digital products. I was well on my way.

Another beautiful discovery that I felt deeply is that this is for everyone. No matter what your passion or calling is in life, digital products can be made to monetize that passion. Cooking, coaching, courses, sports, fitness, relationships, sewing, and the list is endless. No matter what you feel you are called to do, digital products can be made as solutions for other like-minded people.

In this discovery, God gave me clarity about how to best live my purpose and passion: by helping inspire the entrepreneurial spirit in other people, building their dreams, and monetizing their passions.

I took the time to dive deep into who I thought my perfect customer avatar was. I pictured myself 5–10 years ago and decided this person was my avatar. The burned-out working mom who is in desperate need of work-life balance. The woman who lives the after school chaos with sports, cooking, homework and laundry, and then rinses and repeats it the next day. Trying her best to give 100 percent at her job to climb the corporate ladder, gives 100 percent to be a great mom her kids, and 100 percent to friends and spouse. Self-care always falls to the bottom of the list.

This woman feels she is always giving, even giving to the point of not having anything left to give. She may feel that she is not being enough in any aspect of her life because she can't give 100 percent to anything as there is just not enough time in one day. This woman is emotionally exhausted.

What is the "why" behind what you do?

These are the women I am helping, the ones who need time and financial freedom. Those who need to be set free from the emptiness of their 9 to 5 or corporate job that is only robbing them of precious time with the ones they love and having inner peace. I believe each one of us has a specific passion and calling. My goal is to work with my clients to discover this fire inside of them. It is a beautiful thing to witness someone live out their calling. It feels like such an honor to be a part of someone's journey that takes them to where God has called them. Through serving these women and helping them achieve freedom, I am fulfilling my calling.

What is your ultimate impact?

I am so excited for this next chapter of my life. I have created a system that allows people to start and grow the business of their dreams while pursuing their passions. The system I built includes coaching, mindset, accountability, and implementation. It is amazing for someone to be able to monetize their passion with digital products. Living life on your own terms, time, and being financially free is truly achievable. You will have abundance in every way. I am absolutely obsessed with the success of my clients. That is my passion and calling, serving others.

This journey has finally taken away the empty feelings I experienced in Corporate America, leading me to quit that job on December 29th, 2023.

Additionally, I still actively own my firm today and I have had the majority of my clients for over 15 years. My life has been about strong and healthy business relationships and being able to pivot and move forward when you don't think you can. With all of the changes in my life, these relationships have been a pillar for me to lean on. What a gift that I can now assist others to discover their own entrepreneurial spirit and calling and change their lives to achieve financial and time freedom.

I can't think of a bigger change agent than the entrepreneurial spirit. That feeling of wanting something more, wanting your life to look different, and not being satisfied with where you are at today. It's a dream with aligned action. It's who I am to my core. Nothing excites me more than talking about business, and especially when I can help inspire others to create the life and business of their dreams.

I am so grateful for my dad, who ignited this entrepreneurial fire inside of me, and I am so excited to share it with all of you.

How can people connect with you?

I can be found online at https://stan.store/DebbieTheAffiliate and on Instagram @debbie.digital.

WHAT YOU VIBRATE OUT INTO THE WORLD IS PICKED UP AND MIRRORED BACK TO YOU.

Michelle Kaplan

CHAPTER 8

UNCREATING MY REALITY BY MICHELLE KAPLAN

How did I become a warrior to transcend pain? At age 29 I was able to eliminate 12 years of excruciating sciatic pain overnight. I was on a journey to heal my pain naturally because I had gone from doctor to doctor and so-called experts who offered me no advice as to why there was still pain in my back after 12 years. I was tired of waking up limping. I was young, and this pain debilitated me every day since my skiing accident. My hip hurt from the surgery, and I wondered how long my life would be tempered by pain and restrictions. I was on a quest to figure this out.

Then one night, in the course of 24 hours, all the pain and the sciatica disappeared. How was this possible? The night before I had just finished reading a book written by Dr. John Sarno called *Healing Back Pain.* I devoured every word in that book and believed that this was going to be what eliminated my pain. I followed all the instructions to a tee and did exactly what was asked by the author of the book. When I recall this moment years later, waking up the next day to feel absolutely no pain in my body, I am always amazed. It seems miraculous but deep down I know that I was able to manifest it. That experience started the curious obsession I have always had about exploring the connection between the body and the mind.

The most influential book I read when I was 18 was *Unlimited Power* by Tony Robbins. I felt like this book revealed secrets of the human mind. It made me realize that I have the power to alter my thoughts and therefore my reality. Even more profound than that, I learned that when I take control of my thoughts and visualize what I want, those experiences start to come more frequently. I started to experiment with the exercises in the book, and that's when coincidences started to become a normal daily occurrence. I would meet people and instantly they felt so comfortable with me that they started to tell me their deepest darkest secrets. The funny part was they didn't know why.

The more I used the tools in this book, the more coincidences started to happen. One example is when I was starting a promotion company in New York. I was searching for an experienced promoter who could partner with me. Out of all the places and the millions of people in NYC, the exact person I was searching for walked up to me and introduced themself. That partnership lasted several years, and I consider that person to be one of the most influential mentors of my business career. I don't consider any of these occurrences random.

I also learned that there really are no coincidences. We vibrate at a certain frequency. Our thoughts and desires are on a frequency wave. The more we desire them, the more they manifest themselves. At the time I didn't really understand this power, but today I do. It's like tuning into a channel on the radio. If you choose a certain number, you will only get that station. Just like thoughts. If you're thinking about a certain scenario, it will eventually reach you. It's a universal law. Vibrations that resonate at a similar frequency will eventually meet each other. Of course I didn't know all this back then, but I was still doing it regardless because I was deeply desiring the outcome of my thoughts.

Flash forward to 2020. There was a lot of confusion in the world. Somehow, my body had a mind of its own. It decided to stay frozen from my ribs to my abdomen. This made it impossible to lift my arms or even walk or breathe without excruciating pain. I was bedridden and not one doctor could tell me why. After two MRIs, numerous X-rays and blood tests, everything still came back as normal! I had no choice but to go within to heal my own body ... with my mind.

I had a coaching background, so I was fortunate enough to tap into many modalities I had used in the past to shed old traumas. I started to un-create my current situation. I asked some vital questions: What did my body need to shed, purge, and give up to heal itself? What was blocking my energy in order to heal? What thoughts and beliefs were held in my energetic body that were not serving me? What did I have to lose to gain more function, more mobility, more space, and more room in my body to bring it back into balance? These questions became daily mantras I would ask every day. Some days were better than others, as I had massive pain throughout a six-month period.

What did I possibly do for months with no mobility? Part of my everyday routine was researching as much as I could about natural remedies. By this time, I had already included services from energy workers like Reiki, remote energy healers, acupuncture, Chinese herbs, I even had a Shaman at my house! I was searching for anything that could bring me back to balance.

One of the newer modalities I came across was the EESystem or Energy Enhancement System. This is a technology I remember seeing years ago, and it resurfaced just at the right time. It's based on vibrational waves of scalar energy. Developed in the mid-1970s by Dr. Sandra Rose Michael, it was recently released to the general public. I researched the scientific data on the EESystem and was completely amazed. The technology produces naturally occurring waves existing in nature that vibrate at such high levels that they move in and out of dimensions.

As challenging as it is for some people to understand, to me it was the holy grail in quantum physics. There was so much to learn, and the more I researched, the more miracle stories of healing I uncovered. All ailments seemed to align when exposed to this enhanced energy: broken bones, neuropathy, MS, autism, brain issues, heart issues. What was important to understand was that I was the one who healed myself, and the technology provided the environment. I was so excited at the possibilities that I immediately booked a 20-hour block of sessions at an EESystem Center. I set my intention that this experience was going to be the pivotal point in my healing!

Upon arriving at the center, I was very hopeful and determined. I met a lot of people just like myself, who had been searching for another modality to help heal after conventional ways had not worked. When I walked into the wellness room, I was immediately mesmerized by 24 beautiful computer monitors that looked like colorful fuzzy snow. These screens are all calibrated to each other, and when they communicate, they release a charge of hyper healthy scalar and biophotonic waves. This is the electrical charge that is felt. I sat down and reclined in a comfy chair. I closed my eyes and immediately felt a comforting energy envelope me. I was told if I slept, I would get the best experience. My body felt warm and tingly. After an hour I fell into a deep sleep.

When I woke up four hours later, I felt an invigorating rush of energy. My body felt lighter. It was relaxed but energized at the same time. I knew something had changed within me, but I couldn't express exactly what it was. After returning to the center for four straight days, I had significant improvements. The brain fog I had been experiencing was gone. My thoughts were super clear! My eyesight upgraded, and I no longer needed my reading glasses. Most importantly, my body pain was over 50 percent eliminated, and I was able to take a deep breath with less pain than when I had arrived. It felt like a miracle, but it was all science! Quantum physics to be precise.

I learned as much as I could while I was at the Center. The most important thing we can do for our body is to keep our cells at a high vibration. This allows them to communicate with each other and transfer information through the body. When we are in the EE vortex, the cells are being charged. Cellular charge is measured in millivolts. When you raise your millivolt charge, you can power up every cell and allow the body to work optimally. The higher your millivolts the less dis-ease can take residence in your body. In today's world, with all the interference from electronic devices and radiation, the

EE technology allows us to recharge our cells daily. It's like plugging yourself back into pure universal energy.

What is the "why" behind what you do?

In 2022 I opened my own EESystem Center in Delray Beach Florida so people could experience the same breakthrough that I did. I named my wellness center Love and Healing Energy because of the universal love that is available for everyone to tap into. There is no vibration more powerful than love. The EESystem really helped shift my physical body, but also transcended my spiritual belief. Since opening, I have seen hundreds of miracles occur. From blindness to seeing, to neurological issues balanced, arthritis disappearing, aneurysms disappearing, and bones healing. Stress, anxiety, and depression have become a symptom of the past for some. The most common testimonial I hear is people saying they have never slept better in their lives after staying for a session. It's so rewarding and warms my heart to be that conduit for other people to experience healing in their lives. This is why I do what I do.

I would urge anyone who is being challenged right now to take some time and sit quietly. Try and listen to your body, any messages, or any thoughts that pop into your head. Often there are signals and messages that we are ignoring. Our world is full of vibration and information fields. In order to tap into the knowledge that surrounds us, we need to stop our busy minds. This is why meditation is so important to healing. The body has a chance to relax and surrender to another side of information we don't always have access to.

I have learned that you have a choice what to believe and how to heal. Most people have put a label on their issues, like saying, "I have a tumor." If you can strip away the belief that you have or own this symptom, you have a better chance of erasing it. Why would you want to have a tumor, for example? If, on the other hand, you say "my body is experiencing a temporary imbalance, which I will start to balance," you have just opened another avenue for yourself to heal.

As soon as you offer possibilities into your realm, more possibilities show up. Once again, it's that ask and receive universe. The more information you ask for, the more that shows up. If we can un-create what we have always been led to believe, we can un-create our reality and create something new.

This goes for anything in our lives. How our bodies function, the relationships we are in, what we do for work, were all created from an idea or an ideal of how it ought to be. If you ever feel like you are stuck in any direction of your life, you can always change it by changing your mind.

One of my goals is to empower people about their choices. When you are healing yourself, you have a choice. What modalities have you not tried? Some may be as simple as the words you are saying to yourself. Your cells have consciousness; they actually respond to the words you speak and the thoughts you think. When you say words like can't or won't, your body will believe what you say. But if you feed your conscious cells with positive reinforcement, they will respond in kind. Some of the words I use are, "I am balanced," "I am whole," "I am perfect." When I started to believe that I was going to heal myself no matter what, that's when the healing sped up.

What life lessons have created the most growth for you?

I didn't know what was going on in my body, and I didn't have the capacity at the time to try and figure it out. The only option I had was to just let go and believe that there was a life force greater than myself that was going to help me. I don't consider myself religious, but I do believe in a creator. I also believe that we hold a part of the creator within us. I started to call upon this part of me to help me heal. My belief in the creator reinforced my ability to heal myself. I have the power within me to make this happen. I just needed to believe it.

At times this was challenging, but I kept praying and believing. I developed a daily protocol to rid myself of pain. I started with meditation every day, calling on the One Energy of the Universe to bring in white light and replace and dispel dark matter. I flushed my body with high-quality water and lemon juice. I had a conversation with my higher self to balance energy through each chakra. I placed crystals around my body to bring in more energy. When I needed to release emotions, I would cry about old traumas just to purge any blockages. I lost my ego. I didn't want to be in control; I wanted the universal life force to pull negative energy out of me and replace it with light. An important life lesson I learned is that I am a much more powerful being than I could have ever imagined. I can create and re-create anything if I believe in it. Belief and mindset is the key, And also believing in those things which at the time may seem impossible.

Paradigm Shift

After this experience I started to see life in a different light. I understood with my mind that changing your state was possible, but now I had done it several times. My entire world started to look different. I started to feel more powerful than before. I believe that anything is possible with the power of the mind. I started to unravel the traditional ways we look at our lives. Most people think that life works in a systematic norm. We grow up, we work, we save, we vacation, we retire, and we die. I started to view these everyday beliefs as being false. I started to question the narrative that is fed to us from the masses. Did you ever question where you got most of your beliefs from? What if we were universal beings having a human experience? What if we were living miracles? What if we have the power to change our existence and circumstances whenever we desired?

I used visualization. When I could not physically move, I imagined that I could. I saw myself playing tennis, working out, being 12 again, and running very fast. The mind does not know the difference between real and imaginary. Every day started to get better and better, and my pain subsided. I believed I was not in pain, and my body listened to me. Amazing but true.

What is your ultimate impact?

I believe this is a natural progression of my life that I was called to fulfill at this time. Sometimes I feel as if I am being guided by a force greater than myself. I am grateful that each day I wake up with a passion to empower someone else. My ultimate impact would be to alter people's perception about wellness. If I can heal myself twice, I know anyone can heal themselves.

Being well starts with your thoughts. What you vibrate out into the world is picked up and mirrored back to you. It is one of the universal laws. If more people would focus on the positive aspects instead of looking for the negative, they would create more positive experiences. The human belief system is probably the most powerful asset you have.

I have demonstrated that you can go outside your belief system to elicit positive results. You have the ability to tap into a universal field of energy that exists within our stratosphere and beyond. Once you can go beyond what you see, touch, and smell, you open a new world of possibilities. For those people who don't believe it is possible, I urge you to read any book by Dr. Joe Dispenza, who has been doing this type of work for many years. He has scientifically proven that the quantum field of information and the power of thought can alter the physical body. The modalities I used to heal myself are similar to what he has scientifically proven to be true. You have all the power within yourself to make any changes that you want to make in your life. Today there are so many doctors and scientists conducting research in the quantum field; we all have the opportunity to learn how to access this information. My ultimate goal is to get this information out to the masses, allow people to become their own healers, and for people to realize they are much more powerful than they ever imagined.

How can people connect with you?

I can be found at www.loveandhealingenergy.com and on Instagram @loveandhealingenergy.

IT'S NEVER TOO LATE TO TAKE ACTION TOWARD CREATING YOUR OWN UNIQUE, LIVING AND BREATHING LEGACY WHILE YOU STILL HAVE TIME ON THIS EARTH.

Kathy Mela

CHAPTER 9

NOBODY GETS OUT OF THIS LIFE ALIVE
BY KATHY MELA

When I was 19, one of my cousins was murdered. I remember the shock and the sadness, but mostly, I remember the silence. Her name, Peggy, was only spoken in hushed whispers. They found the man who murdered her at the tender age of 14, but no one ever talked about what happened. I didn't understand how to navigate my feelings around this kind of tragedy.

When I was 15, one of my cousins was killed in a motorcycle accident. My aunt lived about 10 miles from us in South Florida, and my cousin was in North Carolina. In 1969 there were no cell phones. My aunt had recently moved to Florida and didn't have a phone yet, so my father got the call around 10:30 pm.

In those days no one called much after 9:00 pm unless it was urgent, so I sensed it was not good news. It was the police in North Carolina. Jimmy had been killed in a motorcycle accident. My parents and I drove to my aunt's home to give her the news. My dad knocked on the door and my aunt opened it. She saw the look on his face and without a word she immediately fainted. My dad caught her as she crumpled to the floor.

Although I'd experienced grief in my life before this, I was struck by the intensity of her reaction, slapped hard by the reality of tragedy and loss. The other losses we'd faced in our family were more distant.

This was immediate, stark, and close to home. My family often avoided sorrow, steering clear of negative feelings.

If you've made it to this part of my story, I imagine you are saying something like, "Great story but what does this have to do with impact entrepreneurs?"

Before I became an entrepreneur, I worked as an employee for large corporations in the healthcare industry. I had a lot of amazing, wonderful experiences, but these experiences were where I looked for happiness, joy, and satisfaction. I appeared happy and successful on the outside, but inside I was struggling. I had become an expert on stuffing my emotions. Keeping a tight lid on these emotions caused an internal blindness to the raging struggle of worth and value inside.

Then I stumbled into my growth journey, which led to my retirement career as a life legacy coach. I started doing the internal work of feeling my emotions and accepting myself as I am. In my mid-50s, for the first time, I began to learn how to feel and how to do the inner work of finding joy.

At first it felt like another thing that I had to do to start feeling emotions. It often felt like a sucker punch to the gut. Stuffing my feelings had left me feeling numb inside. When we block out the pain of grief and loss, we also block our ability to feel other emotions, like love and joy. Taking steps to feel, to be intentional with my life, and to embrace and embody my purpose felt uncomfortable because I was living in a resistant state of being. Little by little I started making changes in my life. I learned to love and value myself as I am. I renewed my sense of purpose.

I came to realize that these two death experiences were the foundation of a belief that the acceptable way to deal with grief was to stuff it.

Experience the Journey

Over the years, I became so good at stuffing my feelings that I went into the medical field. The nursing and medical communities are full of people who care for others but learn to compartmentalize their own emotions in order to function professionally.

While I attended nursing school in college, I worked at a state mental hospital in the children's division. In 1973, there was no system to separate children who had behavior issues from those who had more serious mental health challenges. The ways in which we were taught to handle situations with the children would be considered barbaric today.

I was uncomfortable with the methods of treatment, but I didn't speak up. I wasn't equipped to deal with my own feelings much less the feelings of others, especially those with significant mental health challenges.

My decision to become a nurse was based on my experience with the children at that hospital. Initially I chose nursing as a profession with the intention of focusing on mental health care. However, as I advanced in my nursing training, it became clear that this would not be my path. My path would take me on a journey of life experiences related to my purpose.

During my pediatric rotation, I had my first-time experience of being present at the time of a death. I was caring for a three-year-old boy, Tommy, who was in heart failure. It was a very personal experience because I went to high school with his mother.

I watched little Tommy die in his grandfather's arms. I was so moved with the love, care, and attention this man gave his grandson in his last hours and minutes of life. He held him the whole time so that Tommy would feel his love as he slipped away from his tiny earthly body.

For some innate reason, I have never had a fear of death. Actually, the process of death and dying intrigues me. Early in my nursing career, I read the book *On Death and Dying* by Elisabeth Kübler-Ross. That book started me down a path of being intentional about how I cared for patients, especially those with serious illness and those preparing to die. I decided how I wanted to show up as a nurse. Throughout my 45-year career, this *one* decision has had the biggest impact on the legacy I've created. I ask myself, "If it were me or someone I love in that bed, how would I want them to be cared for?"

My first job as a graduate nurse was in the Neonatal Intensive Care Unit (NICU). I wanted to work at a large teaching hospital in South Florida to gain experience. Although I preferred pediatrics, there weren't any open positions. There were, however, positions open in the NICU. A two-week training course was the beginning of my 45-year journey in the NICU.

When people asked me what I did for a living and they heard I worked with babies, they would often say, "Oh, isn't that wonderful! You take care of babies." Yes, it is wonderful. The majority of our babies in the NICU get better and go home. For most parents, giving birth to a baby is one of the happiest moments in life! But for about 10 percent of births, it can become one of the most highly stressful and anxious times when a newborn baby is sick or born prematurely.

During my two-week course, we were taught a great deal about neonatal physiology and the special care our tiny patients needed. We were *not* taught how to communicate effectively with parents about their feelings of grief and loss. When a baby is not born healthy, parents do experience grief and loss, almost as if the baby died. They grieve over the loss of what their ideal image of their birth and baby experience was to be. We nurses were also not taught how to handle our own feelings. Even now, there are many continuing education courses that are mandatory to renew our licenses, but there is no mandatory course on grief, loss, death and dying. I learned about death and dying on the job and through self-education.

As a bedside nurse I was drawn to caring for the babies who were not going to make it home. I loved caring for those newborns and helping their families come to terms with the fact that their child was not going to be given much time on this earth. Within the NICU, I was often referred to as "the death nurse." This may sound haunting or creepy, but to me it was an honorable title. Many of my colleagues preferred not to take care of the dying babies. They were grateful when I volunteered.

I have learned to tap into my ability to offer compassion and empathy to those in pain. I have a unique ability to read people, their energy, their moods, and their feelings while intuitively connecting with what they need in the moment.

Not all of my experiences of caring for babies in the NICU were about death. We had many moments of joy when our babies got better and went home to grow into healthy children and adults.

In the mid-1980s, one of our babies, Taraji, was born extremely premature at 23 weeks gestation. At that time, most babies who were born under 26 weeks gestation did not survive and those who did had major long-term issues. Babies born under 24 weeks rarely, if ever, survived. Many of us who worked at a local hospital in Broward County, Florida had the joy of watching Taraji flourish into adulthood. Her mother brought her back to the NICU graduate reunions. We had the joy of seeing her grow into a beautiful young woman, who returned to volunteer in the NICU at the hospital where she was born. The circle of life is a beautiful thing. Take the time to notice it, observe it, and experience it in a deep and intentional way.

We often became really attached to our NICU babies. One baby from the West Coast of Florida, whose mom was young and only able to visit him occasionally, became our adopted infant. Johnny spent almost eight months in our NICU. He was very sick, born with gastroschisis: his intestines were outside of his body at birth.

Sometimes the intestines can be put back into the body successfully, but with this sweet baby boy, most of his intestines had become necrotic and needed to be removed; this is called short gut syndrome. The downside to this is that the baby is often not able to digest any food. They are fed intravenously with protein and nutrients. Today there are intestinal transplants that are fairly successful but at that time that possibility was not readily available.

Johnny grew up in our NICU, and all our nurses loved and cared for him like he was our own child. We celebrated his six-month birthday with a party. We got him a stroller and wheeled him around the NICU. We brought clothes and toys for him. We hoped that he would get better, but when the body is fed for a long time intravenously, it puts a lot of stress on the liver. Johnny's liver began to fail. We were devastated.

The morning he died, I was working the day shift and came in early. They had been trying to keep him alive all night long. Ultimately, we knew it was futile. That morning we allowed him to die peacefully in my arms. After Johnny's death, I did what I learned to do well. I stuffed my feelings and went about the business of saving lives and raising my own children.

Embrace the Journey

Many years later after Johnny's death, I went back to school to become a neonatal nurse practitioner (NNP). A NICU nurse orchestrates the bedside care of the babies and an NNP works with the physicians to make the decisions about the care.

Within a few years of becoming an NNP, I had two significant experiences with death that brought more awareness to this learned practice of stuffing feelings. My feelings had become like an old-fashioned Dewey decimal system box in a library. The system was once accessed via an actual box with drawers that held index cards of each book and its location in the library.

In my chest sat my own, overstuffed and long neglected Dewey decimal system box of feelings: grief, love, sadness, loneliness, anger, and frustration. When pushed to breaking point, some drawers in the box would splinter and explode into rage. I didn't know how to process my emotions. I didn't allow myself to feel them, but the box would no longer contain them.

In August 2000 my father died from esophageal cancer. In less than 5 months, after several rounds of chemo and radiation, he left his earthly body. For me, it was a physical and emotional whirlwind. In the midst of this, I worked 60 hours a week, drove 3 hours back and forth to Sebring to help my mom as often as I could, cared for my own children, and was preparing my son to attend high school in Tennessee.

I didn't take much time off from work when my dad died. I jumped right back into the land of the living because I really didn't know how to handle my grief. I knew how to help *others* walk through their grief and loss, but I didn't know how to help myself. I understood the concepts but had not yet started to embody them for myself. So I did what I've always done: I stuffed my emotions at work and I stuffed them at home. And a volcano built inside me, threatening to erupt.

When I first became an NNP, I knew there was a great possibility that one day I would have to run a code by myself. I knew that although I had experience in being a participant in a code, it would be very different being the decision-maker in a code. I planned for it by rehearsing how to run a code over and over in my mind. Then, one night it happened. The call came out at 2:06 am. Emergency, a baby needed to be delivered through an abdominal incision called a cesarean section.

Our team was handed a lifeless baby. For 25 long minutes, I led the team as we ran the code. We did everything exactly as I had practiced, breathing and chest compressions. I placed a tube in the baby's airway to breathe air directly into her lungs; we continued chest compressions. I gave emergency medications and fluid through a special intravenous into the umbilical vein, and the team continued breathing and chest compressions. There was *no response* to any of our treatment.

At 25 minutes after birth, the neonatologist arrived. We stopped the code and pronounced the baby dead. We followed the exact protocol to resuscitate a newborn baby, but unfortunately, we were not successful. *I was not successful.* Once again, I stuffed my inconvenient, ragged emotions into that box in my chest. The box was no longer big enough to hold them.

Embody the Journey

At this point in my life, I've witnessed many more babies, children, and adults die. Some were surrounded by loved ones, some were all alone, some were held by family or friends, and some were receiving invasive medical treatment. Some I was privileged to hold as they left their earthly bodies. All these experiences have helped shape my view of life and death.

My career of saving lives and sometimes allowing those lives we saved to exit with grace, love, and peace is a great part of my legacy. The impact I've had on thousands of families and professional colleagues over 45 years is a wonderful gift, a true blessing to have, and yet it has also been a heavy responsibility.

Embarking on my personal growth journey, I undertook the task of unraveling the weighty responsibility housed within the confines of my emotions box. The turning point arrived unexpectedly, not as a seismic explosion, but rather as a pivotal moment marked by the passing of my dear friend, Rita. In the wake of her departure, a profound realization dawned—the fragility and brevity of life. This seemingly simple yet profound insight shattered the carefully constructed walls surrounding my emotions. Rita's death acted as the catalyst, propelling me into a transformative chapter. It compelled me to delve into the delicate art of expressing my deepest emotions, bravely embracing the vulnerability that accompanies such openness.

Many human beings live their lives as zombies, walking around, going through the motions, yet not feeling fulfilled or satisfied inside. Sometimes they even stumble into living a moderately satisfying life. They seek happiness externally when what they are really seeking is already inside of them. It's as if they're the "walking dead." It is my mission in life as an impact entrepreneur to guide these individuals back to living joyfully and passionately. Perhaps that seems ironic, given the fact that I have eased so many others into peaceful deaths. But as an expert in the circle of life, this is my message. It *is* possible to live an immensely satisfying life, here and now, before you depart this earth. And my experience with death has reinforced to me that life is precious.

Each of us has one amazing life to live. I believe that death is not as scary as we think. Life and death do not have to be as hard as we think. There is an abundance of joy, love, peace, and goodness if we choose to see it. Doing the inner work of feeling, our emotions help each of us embody our own unique path and create our own conscious, living, and breathing legacy.

We all have a purpose in life. There is a reason we are here. Sometimes we walk through our lives without clarity of purpose. Although I haven't always understood the steps of my own journey, I intuitively followed a path that led me to uncover my true purpose. My purpose is to radiate love. My legacy is to offer hope for the living and be a light of acceptance and peace for the dying.

The truth is we all have a limited time on this earth. *Nobody gets out of this life alive!* We don't know how long we'll be here—it might be a few minutes, a few days, or a hundred years. When you die, and we all will at some point, what is the legacy you leave behind? Who are you being? What are you doing with your life? Do you want your legacy to be decided by the people at your funeral? Or would you rather intentionally create an immensely satisfying life, where you can slide into home plate shouting, "Wow! What a ride!" knowing that you've made the most of your time on this earthly journey? It's all about the richness of your experiences and the depth of the connections you've made along the way.

"AS YOU NAVIGATE THIS ROLLERCOASTER OF LIFE, MAKE SURE YOU'RE CREATING A STORY WORTH TELLING, ONE FILLED WITH LAUGHTER, TEARS, AND A HEARTY DOES OF MADNESS."
—*Success Minded*

What unique framework or service do you offer to your community or clients?

My unique framework is based on three pillars—experience | embrace | embody intertwining experiences with the willingness to embrace and embody the creation of an intentional legacy.

- Live Full Out—Live life in all its fullness while exploring the experiences that brought you to the present moment
- Enthusiasm—Connect with who you are and how your experiences relate to your purpose and vision for your life legacy
- Gifts—Use Your Gifts—Uncover your gifts to own your value and worth in order to embrace what's really possible in this season of life
- Alignment—Examine why you're here and what holds you back from embracing your best life
- Confidence—Gaining clarity embodies confidence to commit to why you want to be proactive in your living and dying experience
- Yes—Saying yes to yourself means embodying your legacy and inviting more joy, satisfaction, peace, love, and abundance

What life or business lessons have created the most growth for you?

The lesson of self-compassion has created the most impact and growth for me and the people I serve. As a young child, I learned that "selfish is bad." I thought the only other option was being selfless. Selfish is to put your own needs ahead of others, often to their detriment. Selfless is to put others needs ahead of your own, often to your detriment. I realized I didn't want to live in either definition. I call this middle ground "self-compassion," where you recognize and take care of your own needs while considering the impact on others.

This is the essence of my legacy: sharing the importance of conscious legacy creation.

What is your ultimate impact?

My ultimate impact is to bring awareness to the fact that we are finite beings, who have a brief period of time on this earth. I want to encourage people, especially women over 50, to think about their lives and legacies in a way that gets them to take action and explore what's possible when they are proactive about both living and dying. It's never too late to take action toward creating your own unique, living and breathing legacy while you still have time on this earth.

How can people connect with you?

I can be found at kathymela.com and at
https://bit.ly/ConnectWithKathy

TAKE A STEP. AND THEN ANOTHER. AND THEN WALK INTO YOUR BEAUTIFUL TOMORROW.

Mike and Kelly Olive

CHAPTER 10

WHEN FEAR IS BREWING
BY MIKE AND KELLY OLIVE

It was Girl's Mic Night; a special night exclusively for female musicians, spoken word artists, and creatives to empower and encourage girls of all ages. Sights of lights and flowers and the sounds of lattes steaming filled the air. Alonis, an 11-year-old girl who didn't have a shy bone in her body, was excited to perform that night. The stage was where she felt most at home. She was a theater student. As a gifted performer, and it was her turn to be in the spotlight. The music started, and she began to sing. Tonight's musical selection was "Tomorrow," the classic song from the musical *Annie*. As she began to sing, her voice soared in a tone more mature than her young 11 years. With confidence she was delivering her best rendition of this endearing song. The room was captivated and inspired. But then, unexpectedly and much to everyone's surprise, her voice began to quiver and her hands shake. In the middle of the song, her mind suddenly went blank, and she forgot the words. As she approached the climax of the song, the room seemed to grow dim, and time slowed to a melancholy stop. She found herself facing the fear of tomorrow.

The fear of tomorrow is real. Have you ever felt the fear of tomorrow? Maybe out of nowhere when you thought you had a firm footing and then, bam! Maybe it wasn't on a stage singing but in making decisions in life and business. Perhaps when you were on the cusp of tomorrow's next great thing in your life, you just froze. Fear is real, and fear of the unknown is universal to all of us. What we do with that fear is what makes or breaks lives, businesses, and even futures. Let me assure you that facing that fear despite the possibility of failing is worth it. You can face it or flee it. Facing it may result in rewards greater than you could ever imagine.

In 2014, our organization, Common Ground Community Development, encountered an unexpected unknown and decided to face it. We decided to do something we had never done before. With almost no funding, little training, and no previous experience, we looked at those gray clouds, took a leap of faith, and started our first ever social enterprise. We started a coffee shop!

It all began back in 2006 when we started a nonprofit organization to make a difference in our world and help others to give back. We started small, offering instrumental and vocal lessons and classes. Through the years, we grew to over a hundred students. We started a children's choir and began creative enrichment classes for homeschoolers. Our passion was to make a bigger impact in the lives of individuals in our community through programming that was affordable, accessible, professional, and fun. That sounds noble, right? However, professional is often expensive, and affordable and accessible doesn't always pay the bills! We needed a way to generate revenue to support and increase our impact.

Jumping ahead to 2014, we moved our operations to the City of Lake Worth Beach, an artsy coastal town in Southeast Florida. We rented a small bay on a side street. Next door to our little studio was a cute and quirky coffee shop. Coffee and creatives are the perfect blend, so we spent a lot of time in that coffee shop. Live music, local artists' paintings, photos hanging on the walls, and the smell of coffee brewing made this the perfect place for creatives. Alas, much to our dismay, that shop wasn't viable and had to close. This is the moment we got hit with the unexpected fear: could we, as a nonprofit, create a place for the community to gather, musicians to grow and perform, and open a coffee shop? Could this be the answer to increasing our revenue and our impact? Could we really do it? Coffee shops encompass everything that we as an organization of artists and musicians loved—creativity, community, and, of course, coffee! They are a gathering ground for people to work, meet, hang out, create, and find community.

Our driving impact

After much prayer, contemplation, and research, we made the decision to face our unknown and compose our own song. The questions began to flood in. How do we open a coffee shop? What do we do first? What is a POS? What licenses do we need? How will we run it? We had never done anything like that before. We could have had paralysis by analysis at that point. We could have played it safe. But instead, we decided to tackle each task one measure at a time, and in less than two months, we opened Common Grounds Coffee Bar in the heart of the downtown district. This was nothing short of a miracle! Our team and donors came together to work the impossible. To say God had His hand in each step of the process would be an understatement. Donations came in quickly. Volunteers came to paint, build out cabinets, clean, and set up equipment. Staff put in overtime to get things up and running.

In the beginning, the staff were all volunteers. Our vision and desire for a place of community drove us to show up and offer a wonderful experience for our customers. Our customer service and care for people overshadowed our business learning curve. We immersed ourselves in learning all we could to have a flourishing business with amazing coffee. Our fear of the unknown was slowly dissipating.

We began with bare bones equipment. Our espresso machine arrived three days before opening. We made due with used equipment and upgraded as we were able.

As the coffee bar grew, a wonderful yet unexpected impact began to happen. Not only were we able to be a place of common ground for people of all backgrounds, lifestyles, and beliefs to belong, but we now had expanded our nonprofit mission to social entrepreneurship, offering jobs to individuals who had a less than perfect background. We were able to help move them from common ground to higher ground. Job skills, opportunities, and even career paths were being offered. Our impact in our community was crescendoing.

Common Grounds Coffee Bar became the largest revenue producer for our organization and became a go-to place in the City of Lake Worth Beach. Facing our fear of the unknown had far surpassed our expectations, propelling us to more impact than we could have anticipated, and there was no looking back!

In a downtown area dominated by bars, we became a safe and sober place for those in recovery (a huge population in our area) to hang out and host NA and AA meetings. Church groups met there for Bible study. The monthly Utterance Open Mic shows offered a stage to local budding musicians, and the walls of the shop became gallery space for local artists. Our name, Common Ground, was truly our philosophy.

Back to Tomorrow

Stage fright began to grip Alonis as she approached the climax of the song. The hostess of the night heard the fear in her voice and knew she had to do something quick! In a split-second decision, she joined Alonis on the stage, placed her hands on the young singer's shoulders in support, stood cheek to cheek, and began to sing in unison with her. That was when the magic happened. One by one the crowd joined in to sing as a choir until they reached the height of the song. "Tomorrow! Tomorrow! I'll love you tomorrow. You're only a daaaaaaay aaaaaaa-waaaaaay!" The room was electric! The audience exploded and cheered. The girls had helped Alonis face her fear of tomorrow and in doing so, personified empowerment, encouragement, and support. It was one of the most memorable moments of our organization's history.

Since that special day, there have been many more tomorrows. Each tomorrow has connected to the next as we have faced the gray days, challenges, opportunities, frustrations, hurdles, and hope. Through hard work, persistence, growth, and consistency, overcoming our fear of the unknown tomorrows has turned into many years of yesterdays and todays. Common Grounds Coffee Bar has evolved from one small nonprofit community-based coffee shop to Common Grounds Brew and Roastery's three for-profit coffee shops and a coffee roastery. Our son, Justin Olive, has become our business partner and has brought the business and the mission to the next level. Our impact has now grown to over 35 employees with meaningful jobs in a safe and supportive work environment and three welcoming spaces for individuals to continue to gather, work, meet, hang out, and find community and common ground.

Are you facing an unknown tomorrow? Do you have a dream for a better tomorrow? Face your unexpected fear. Take a step. And then another. And then walk into your beautiful tomorrow.

What is the "why" behind what you do?

Our "why" is because of what happens around a table.

- When we sit at a table with one another, we slow down.
- When we sit at a table, we see one another.
- When we sit at a table, we practice listening to one another.
- When we sit at a table to have coffee with someone, it is more than sharing a drink of a green bean roasted to perfection, ground, and brewed to make a comforting cup of coffee. It is a tradition of human history to share with those you love and to wake up the hope of a brand-new day.

The pace of the race of life is faster than ever. Slowing that pace down is important. Sure, there are those who get a cup to go, but even with that, they come into one of the shops each day. And when they do, we know their name, we know their face, and we ask, "Tom, will it be the usual today?" For those who do sit, there is conversation and life shared.

Coffee with people can be shared in a million different ways. Finding that common ground by slowing down and sitting with one another leads us to help others find their "whys."

When we sit with one another, we see one another, really see one another, and the distance between assumptions and realities begins to narrow. As we practice listening, our understanding grows.

As current culture fractures and divides, people are looking for community. They are looking for a safe space, a third place, a place of common ground. We are cultivating spaces for people from all walks of life to be able to walk into, feel seen, and belong.

Our "why" is also for our employees. We coach them to help them climb, to find upward mobility through personal growth and being a part of a healthy team, and to develop leadership skills to help them to grow and to learn how to give back—all of this offers a ladder to higher ground. Lastly, through the social entrepreneurship programs of our nonprofit, we are helping businesses grow and give back through networking and coaching. When businesses grow and give back, communities flourish.

What life or business lessons have created the most growth for you?

Lessons in life and business are often synonymous because they are always about people. Having the right people on your team and in your life is the hinge on which the door of success swings. Here are some lessons that have created growth for us:

1. Never underestimate people. Sometimes, all they need is a little encouragement and training to flourish and shine.
2. Like coffee, life and business is a process. Genesis 8:22 talks about seed time and harvest. Between the beginning of your business (seed) to profitability (harvest), there is time. Trust

the process. Don't rush the process. Work the process. Enjoy the process.

3. It's not always about the money, but you've gotta have to have it to keep on going! Value what you do and value your team.

What advice would you give to someone considering entrepreneurship?

1. Persistence, consistency, and diligence are the trifecta of a thriving business. The landscape of business is constantly evolving. There are thriving seasons and down seasons. Stay the course. Don't be the one who stops two steps shy of their payoff. If we had quit early on, we would have missed out on the impact we have made in our community.

2. Adapt to changes in your field. The old adage rings true: the only thing that stays the same is change. What worked last year, last month, or even last week may not work today. Pivot. Adjust. Be flexible.

3. Look for creative solutions. This is probably one reason you went into business in the first place! Think outside the box and don't feel like you have to stick to the traditional way of doing things.

4. Take time to build your foundation and infrastructure well. It's not fun or sexy, but it will pay off in dividends when you do. Build your website. Establish your email address. Get a business card. Set up your systems and work them.

5. Have an accurate vision of what it is you want to do. Then plan out how you want to do it. You have to see it before you do it. Realize that there are things that can obstruct your vision and practice looking beyond the obstruction. Sometimes this can include getting another pair of eyes on it to possibly see things you might not be seeing.

6. Don't wait until you know everything to get started! This thing called business is like an open-book test. Learn as you go.
7. Don't do it alone. One really is the loneliest number. Team really does accomplish more. Get your team—your right team—and do it together.
8. Seek counsel. In the book of Proverbs 24:6 in the Bible, it says that there is wisdom in a multitude of counselors. Look for and lean on those who have gone before you on this journey. They can help you avoid pitfalls and potholes along the path.
9. Be a solution finder and problem-solver. What problem can you solve or solution can you find for your customer? How can you serve them and add value to them?
10. Pray. Can't figure out the answer to a situation in your business? Pray. Stumped? Pray. Confused? Pray. Struggling with a decision? Pray. Need new creative ideas or solutions? Pray. He listens and answers!

What is your ultimate impact?

Our ultimate impact is connecting with people through common ground to help them take steps to higher ground. Connecting with others to add value to their lives and make it better fuels us. We do it through coffee, community, social entrepreneurship, and the arts. When our fractured and divided world can find some common ground, sit at a table, and share a cup of coffee, we can begin to make impact in the lives of those around us.

How can people connect with you?

We can be found at www.cglakeworth.org and on Instagram @commongroundsbr.

IT'S ALL ABOUT GETTING STARTED. IT'S THAT SIMPLE, AND IT'S THAT HARD.

Dr. Breanna Smith Powderly

CHAPTER 11

ENTREPRENEURSHIP, PLATE SPINNING, AND GETTING STARTED
BY DR. BREANNA SMITH POWDERLY

E ven as a little girl, I knew what I was doing.

It all started at home. You see, my dad was a chiropractor who owned his own practice, so from a young age, I got to see him care for people and run a small business: a firsthand example of what entrepreneurship looked like. That was what planted the seed.

As I got older, I worked a lot of different jobs, but I knew they were only a temporary means to an end. One day, I was going to be my own boss running my own business. In my mind, there really was no other option—it never even occurred to me that I would work for anybody but myself.

I *knew* that this was my calling. And I *knew* what I was doing.

So I followed in my dad's footsteps. I went to chiropractic school, got good grades, graduated early, and set out on my journey to begin my career of bringing healing to families. I was on the younger side when I graduated and got my license, but I was so confident about my ability to analyze someone's spine, adjust them appropriately, and help them get better.

I *knew* what I was good at, and I *knew* what I was doing!

So at twenty-three years old, passionate, motivated, and beyond excited to get my chiropractic practice started, I walked into the bank to take the first step toward opening my own business.

"My name is Dr. Breanna," I said confidently. "I'm here to open up my business bank account."

"Great!" said the woman at the bank. "I just need your DBA and your EIN."

"Um…" I said. "My what?"

"Your DBA and your EIN," she said.

I stared at her. I knew every vertebra of the human spine. I knew every muscle. I had studied every nerve that exited the spine and where it went in the body. But I had no clue what this lady was talking about. Here I was, trying to start my own business, and not only did I not *have* my DBA or my EIN, but I had never even heard those abbreviations before (by the way, they stand for Doing Business As and Employment Identification Number. You're welcome).

It was at that moment that it occurred to me for the first time, *Oh, crap. Maybe I actually don't know what I'm doing…*

More challenges along the way

From that day forward, I sought out help anywhere I could find it. I talked to people at the bank to learn the basics. What was a sole proprietorship? How did that differ from an LLC? I spoke to colleagues and chiropractors about their businesses. How do you get patients to come in? More importantly, how do you get them to come back? And I did a lot of my own research. How do you pay taxes? And, oh yeah, how do you pay yourself?

These were just a few of the things nobody had ever taught me.

In the beginning, I didn't even know what I didn't know. I made mistakes. I made mistakes filing paperwork. I ran into all sorts of challenges. And, not surprisingly, some days were rougher than others.

I distinctly remember what may have been my lowest moment. I was only a month or so into my practice, but I'd made some progress, and things were starting to look up. Like all new chiropractors ready to change the world, I was a starry-eyed optimist, convinced that I would throw open my doors, and people would come rushing in for me to help them.

I remember sitting in my office one late afternoon, alone. I only had three people scheduled to come in that evening, but I was excited to help them. Those three people were going to get the most exceptional care they'd ever had!

Time ticked by, and the first patient didn't show up.

Huh, I thought. *Well, that's okay. It happens to everyone.*

I waited. And the second patient didn't show up, either.

Okay, not great, I thought. *But life goes on. This last patient is still going to get the most exceptional care of their life!*

I sat in my office through the evening, waiting for the third patient … who also never showed up.

All three of my scheduled clients that evening were no-shows. I'll never forget sitting there, behind the front desk of the business I had started, alone in my office, crying.

That night, it really hit me how much harder this was than what I'd expected it to be. In fact, I started to wonder if I should rethink this whole thing. Maybe I would be better off working for someone else after all. It wasn't too late to switch career paths. I could get another job. Or I could sort of meet in the middle and bartend on the side to make ends meet.

I didn't know it at the time, but this was a key moment for me. It's a key moment that all entrepreneurs face when that little voice in your head says, "Are you sure this is really what you're supposed to be doing?" It's at this point that the entrepreneur is forced to choose whether she is going to compromise on her vision or go all in on it despite the setbacks. For me, the answer was clear. I had to *make* this work because I knew it was what I was meant to do. Compromising wasn't an option.

That night was a definite low point, but I told myself to get back up, push the doubt I felt to the side, and keep moving. The only way this was going to work was if I gave it my single-minded focus.

What is the "why" behind what you do?

At the time of writing, I've now been in practice as a chiropractor for six and a half years. I've created a thriving, successful business from scratch. I've built a close-knit family of patients whom I have the privilege of caring for on a regular basis. And I'm also proud to say that I've made an impact in my community.

All in all, I think it's safe to say that I've come a long way since that first day at the bank.

In my office, doing consistently incredible work and providing exceptional care, especially to women and families, is a huge part of my brand. It's what my clients know they'll get from my business every time they walk in the door because it's what I feel they deserve. And I get to provide it to them every single day. It's my goal, my calling, and the "why" behind everything I do in my career.

But it didn't happen overnight.

I certainly wasn't the first new chiropractor to face the problem I encountered that day at the bank. Because the funny thing about chiropractic is you don't only have to be a chiropractor; you have to be a business owner, too. Many of us feel like graduating from chiropractic school and getting our license is the culmination of all our hard work. You go to school for all those years, and when it's over and done with, you're so eager to get out there and help people. But then you realize, "Wait, now I have to build a business from the ground up. Nobody taught me to be an entrepreneur! What am I supposed to do?"

Like I said, I grew up knowing that I would one day be my own boss. Sounds great, right? But the thing is, being your own boss doesn't mean you don't have a boss. What it really means is that you actually have to be your own boss (And a lot of us spend our days dealing with troublesome employees…).

As your own boss,

1. **You are the manager**. You set the schedule and make sure you show up to work.
2. **You are the supervisor**. You set expectations, and you hold yourself accountable for what gets done.
3. **You are quality assurance**. You ensure that you meet the standards you have set for the quality of work you produce.
4. **You are entry-level staff**. How you do one thing is how you do everything. And depending on where you are in your entrepreneurial journey, it may be up to you to take out the trash, organize your workspace, and get the office ready for work tomorrow.
5. **You are human resources**. You are in charge of training yourself in all the areas in which you need to be educated in order to do your job.

Notice how many times I just used the word "you"?

It was that final role listed above, training and education, that *I* had to step into as a twenty-three-year-old, newly licensed chiropractor. That day at the bank was a wake-up call. Sure, I knew how to do the work, but I didn't know the first thing about running a business—yet!

Okay, so I don't know what I'm doing, I thought. *Am I going to let that stop me?*

I can do this! How hard can it be?

What life or business lessons have created the most growth for you?

My story is just one example of how for every hundred things you need to learn about your field as an entrepreneur; there are about a thousand other things you will also have to learn that you aren't even aware of yet.

I'm grateful that I didn't know what I didn't know because it gave me the opportunity to take a leap of faith and learn as I went. When it comes to advice in personal and professional development, I often hear people refer to the "work/life balance." They talk about it as if it's a seesaw, with work on one side and life on the other. This is a particularly common talking point among women who get started on their entrepreneurial journeys and quickly discover how challenging it is to meet the demands of running a business, taking care of their families, raising their kids, etc. "It's all about finding that balance," people will tell you, as if you're just a few simple changes away from perfect harmony. Personally, I don't think this is a good analogy at all.

One of the most important lessons I learned on my journey was that it was less about finding balance than it was about spinning plates. As an entrepreneur, you are a plate spinner, and you can expect to have seven or eight different metaphorical plates spinning all at once. On those plates are labels like *business, kids, spouse, health, friends, marketing, me time,* and the list goes on.

So, how do you keep these plates spinning? By knowing where, at any given time, to prioritize your focus and your energy. For example, there are going to be times when the *business* plate is spinning nicely, but the *spouse* plate is starting to look a little wobbly. That's your sign to redirect focus from your business for a little while and prioritize your relationship with your spouse to get that plate spinning again. Or maybe you're doing great in most categories, but you've been neglecting your health and fitness. Time to get that plate's RPMs back up by redirecting your focus toward it for a while. Overall, your job is to stay keenly aware of which plates require your attention at any given time. And, full disclosure, I haven't always been the best at this.

When I first started my business, it was literally just me. It used to be that I was the chiropractor, I was the girl at the front desk, I did all the scheduling, I did the billing, and if you called the office, I was the one who answered the phone. I knew everyone's names and birthdays and what was going on in their lives.

I liked the intimate environment I had created. I genuinely enjoyed the fact that I was able to give a personal touch to everybody who walked through my doors. That's probably why so many chiropractors start out with this same setup and never move past it, often having a spouse run the front desk and answer the phones or maybe hiring one assistant to help out if needed.

One of the hardest parts of being an entrepreneur is learning to adjust to growth when you get too big to keep those plates spinning all on your own.

Today, we have three chiropractors working at two offices with two front desks. And while this is great, it kills me sometimes that I don't have those special connections with everyone like I used to. I have to remind myself that thanks to the amazing team I've built and the culture we've created here, I can be confident that the people who enter my offices receive that same love, attention, and exceptional care, even if it doesn't come from me personally.

There is no work/life seesaw. And there is no magic center point, where if you get things just right, your life will be in balance. You're the boss. You have to decide where your attention is required. And when you get pushback from the employee side of your brain, make sure the boss wins.

As you move through life's ups and downs, your energy reserves will vary. There may be times when *all* your plates start looking wobbly. Fortunately, these plates ain't your mom's antique china. If you drop one, they rarely break. Just pick it back up and get it spinning again.

What advice would you give to someone considering entrepreneurship?

If I could give a few pieces of advice to someone considering entrepreneurship, it would be the following:

Get Started

It's all about getting started. It's that simple, and it's that hard.

People get so wrapped up in their own stories and so self-conscious about their decisions that they self-sabotage. Their desire to figure out every little detail and build the perfect plan before taking action puts an end to their journey before it can even begin. Believe me, I understand. We all want to feel that we've done everything we can possibly do to prepare for the journey ahead. But the harsh reality is you're never going to feel ready. You're never going to feel confident. You're never going to feel like the timing is right. But you have to get started anyway. It's like jumping off a high diving board for the first time. You don't stop being afraid. You feel the uncertainty, and you take the leap in spite of it.

My advice is just get started. You don't have to know every little detail. You can figure it out as you go.

Don't Be Afraid to Change Your Mind

As you progress on your journey and figure things out, it's okay to change your mind!

From the perspective of the traditional working world, this is a difficult concept to understand. *Change your mind? Never! If you start something and then decide not to finish it, it means you failed at it!*

This thinking could not be more wrong.

Allow me to be the first to give you permission: you are allowed to change your mind. You're in charge. (And nobody's keeping score anyway.)

Build Relationships

And finally, as you learn and grow, don't just focus on building your business; focus on building relationships.

To clarify, I'm not talking about networking through inauthentic experiences. This goes beyond trading business cards. I'm talking about growing a rock-solid community of like-minded people.

As the owner of a largely family-based practice, I've developed relationships with midwives, doulas, pediatric dentists, and many other specialists whom I regularly refer patients to, and they often refer patients to me, too. This didn't manifest because I walked into their offices and said, "Hey, here's who I am, here's what I do, and here's my card. Please send people to me." That approach might work once in a while, but quite frankly, it's just tacky. It's transparent, it's blatantly self-serving, and it doesn't feel good for anyone involved.

Instead, I walk into their offices and ask, "Who are you? What do you do? How can I send people to you, and how can we help serve the same population together?" I can't tell you how many times I've done this and gotten responses like, "Oh, my gosh! That would be great! This could be a really great relationship because we've been looking for a chiropractor to send people to."

There's a lot of really bad entrepreneurship advice out there. Things like, "You've got to get out there and sell yourself! It's all about the hustle!" But when you're inauthentic, people can smell it from a mile away. They can sense whether you're truly trying to help others or just trying to help yourself.

The same goes for the patients who are under my care. I don't do the hard sell. I don't pressure people to bring their entire families in so I can build my practice. Instead, the real, genuine, loving relationships I've built with my patients have led to organic growth. I don't have to feel weird about it because it all happens naturally.

Whatever business you're building, remember that you're not just building the business. You're building relationships fueled by the desire to help people, and you have to communicate that desire authentically from your heart.

What is your ultimate impact?

I truly love my patients. There are times when I can't sleep at night because I'm lying awake wondering how they are, how their families are doing, and what I can do to help them. I want to see them heal, grow, and thrive. And just as my business has organically grown, so has my calling to serve people.

Having built a successful business and learned about how to navigate through many of the challenges along the way, I've realized that I can help people not only through chiropractic, but through some business advice as well.

Here are my main tips on how to get started:

Define Your Why. What are you passionate about? Why are you passionate about it? Why do you want to share that passion with others? What about this excites you?

Decide What You Want. What does a day in your dream life look like? How does this day feel to you? How does it feel to imagine it? If it currently feels impossible or far-fetched, why do you think you feel that way?

Figure Out Who You Want to Serve. Who is your dream client? Why do you feel passionate about this client? What problems do they have? How can you solve one or more of those problems for them?

If you take anything away from this chapter, I hope it will be this: You don't have to know everything first in order to get started. You can figure it out along the way. And no matter what setbacks you may encounter, whether it's a rude awakening at the bank or some no-show clients, it's not over until you decide it is.

Everything is figure-outable.

So go get started.

How can people connect with you?

I can be found at www.lifeadjustedchiro.com and on Instagram @drbreannapowderly.

IT IS ONLY IN THE FACE OF ADVERSITY THAT OUR TRUE STRENGTH OF CHARACTER IS REVEALED.

Wendy Shore

CHAPTER 12

IMPACT ON PURPOSE, DRIVEN TO SUCCEED BY WENDY SHORE

MY STORY IS NOT UNIQUE, BUT IT'S UNIQUELY MINE.

—*Wendy Shore*

I had a good childhood growing up in a loving, working-class family. My parents sacrificed to make sure my sister and I never went without. As of the writing of this chapter, I still have both of my parents. I am blessed.

For a long time I struggled with the notion that my story needed a clear hero's journey moment to be compelling. Marketers say stories sell, requiring a pivotal event that sets the hero on their path. Have I faced difficulties and challenges in my life? Absolutely. Only by overcoming obstacles can inner strength be discovered, and sometimes in the process, an unexpected new path is revealed.

My journey here has been a series of paths taken. Sometimes I took the wrong path, and I had to double back. I've made mistakes and bad decisions. I've done wrong things with good intentions. But through it all, I kept moving forward. There was no single defining moment, just an accumulation of experience, challenges overcome, and lessons learned along each path.

Success and personal growth are not exclusively reserved for those who experience dramatic, life-altering events. That does not make you or your story any less valuable or significant. You don't need to wait for a grand, defining moment to feel worthy. You can be successful and make an impact simply because you set out to do so.

Things came relatively easy to me. In school, I didn't really have to study. I was a great test taker, and I passed the CPA exam on the first try. I tell you this not to boast, but rather to give you a glimpse into my mindset.

When things come easily, there are valuable lessons missed along the way. It can sometimes lead us to shy away from challenges, missing out on the growth and resilience that come from facing and overcoming adversity.

I've always known that I would be in business for myself. I was just 14 years old when the condo next door to us went up for sale. I told my parents they should purchase it, rent it, and someday pass it on to me (stating boldly that I would be living right next door to them, as if that were a selling point). Somehow. I recognized it as an investment opportunity. I envisioned building a real estate empire, but I was 14 years old; it would have to wait.

At 15 I went to work at a restaurant called Ponderosa. I loved working in a restaurant. I was ambitious and relished coming up with new ideas. My ambition only grew from there. As I served customers, I observed the nuances of the business, absorbing lessons that would prove invaluable in my future ventures.

When I graduated from high school, all my friends were heading off to college, but I decided to stay local and go to Rockland Community College (RCC) so I could begin my real estate career. I majored in business, excelling in the classes, especially accounting. Meanwhile, I patiently waited to turn 18 so I could take the real estate license exam. The moment finally arrived. I passed the exam and secured a job at a local real estate office, thrilled to dive into the industry that I'd envisioned building my career.

My excitement quickly met a harsh reality.

I was paired with a cantankerous veteran agent, who believed I was too young and too green (and too female) for this business. He bluntly stated how hard it would be for me, and that nobody would want to work with someone so young. Definitely not wanting to mentor me, his cynicism and criticism left me discouraged.

Accustomed to things coming easily, I was caught off guard by the need to push for what I desired. Rather than push forward or prove him wrong, I simply walked away from my dream, missing the chance to learn important lessons that come from persevering.

The easy path rarely aligns with our aspirations; it's pushing through challenges that forges growth and success.

I continued working toward my degree and got a job at a stereo store, where I met a guy who I really thought I was going to marry. When the semester ended we went on vacation together to London. It was the first time I had been out of the country, and I was in awe.

It was so different from anything I had experienced. I spent a great deal of time in New York City, but London was different. It had a different vibe. The shops were different, and there were a variety of things that were just unavailable in the States, unlike today where you can pretty much get anything you want from anywhere in the world, (and often within two days).

While sitting in Queen Mary's Rose Garden, I looked across a field at a university and thought how nice it would be to go to school in London. Upon returning home, I mentioned it to my parents who did some research and found that RCC had a program where I could spend a semester in London. They felt I should take the opportunity.

I was initially excited and then I was hesitant; I had never been away from home for that long, and I didn't want to leave my boyfriend behind.

I had a very big decision to make. Do I take the chance and go? I was scared that my stomach was in knots, but I knew that if I didn't go now, I would never have the opportunity again. I left my family, friends, and boyfriend and went back across the pond to Ealing London College of Higher Education.

Opportunities do not always present themselves; you must be prepared when they do. I felt the fear and did it anyway.

It was probably the best experience of my life. I met a wonderful group of friends from back home, who were also attending Ealing College. Many of them were studying hospitality, and since my first job was in the restaurant industry, we had much in common. Together we visited many pubs and restaurants and went to the theater. I immersed myself in London living.

As my time in London was ending, my new friends were going to travel around Europe. They wanted me to join them, but I'd already been gone too long from my boyfriend. We had made plans for our future, and that future with him awaited. I bid them farewell and went home to pack. While packing, my boyfriend called me long distance to tell me he would not be meeting me at the airport—he met someone while I was away.

I was coming home to a life I planned, but fate had decided it had other plans for me. I was devastated! I also just turned down an opportunity to travel the world.

That moment stands as a reminder that safety can hold us back from seizing opportunities. It's those leaps into the unknown that often yield the greatest rewards.

After spending all that time with my friends in the UK, I decided that I should go into hospitality. After all, I loved my restaurant job, and I really had a knack for it.

I turned 20, graduated college, and I got my dream job as the assistant food and beverage manager for the Sheraton Hotel. I was so excited. What an opportunity!

Except it wasn't.

Challenges quickly arose as the general manager seemed to be in a relationship with my direct boss and took issue with the amount of time I spent around him. She was determined to make my life miserable and undermined me at every turn. I spent a lot of time doing paperwork and little time working with guests. I found myself in a job that didn't quite align with my aspirations. My initial enthusiasm quickly faded. I was miserable. I was falling short of my potential.

Recognizing when a chosen path isn't leading to the desired destination is a crucial part of personal and professional growth.

Too many people stay on a path they initially chose even when they realize it's not the right fit for them. Financial security, lack of confidence, fear of change, as well as commitment bias can hold them back.

Now what? I had friends who were majoring in accounting. I thought about my own aptitude for the subject and returned to school, ultimately graduating with a BBA in accounting. To pay for school, I worked various restaurant jobs: hostess, server, bartender, even washing dishes if needed. I enjoyed it, and it paid the bills.

I passed the CPA exam and started at Ernst and Young upon graduation. I was learning a lot and adding to my growing skill set. I loved the work, but I did not love the corporate hierarchy. Some managers acted disrespectfully toward first years, subjecting them to hazing-like treatment of fraternity pledges. My manager exemplified this, offering me my first insight into the difference between management and leadership.

While working at Ernst and Young, I was assigned to an audit in Allendale NJ. There was an Italian restaurant in the shopping center, and as it turns out, it was owned by a chef that I had worked with. It was here that I met my now ex-husband; he was one of the partners. Funny enough, we lived in the same town 20 miles away. I knew his brother, but not him. They were short-handed in the restaurant and asked me to help them out. Although initially hesitant, in no time I was working there 5–6 nights a week. It turns out I have a genuine passion for the restaurant industry. In retrospect, it seems what I did not like was the hotel business and the corporate structure. Accounting degree and CPA certification in hand, I wound up right back in the restaurant business.

Embrace serendipity & chance encounters

That unexpected detour reinforced my passion. I opened my first restaurant with my now ex-husband in 1991. It was a great learning experience doing everything from lease negotiations, collaborating on architectural plans, decorating, selecting smallwares, designing the menu, creating a wine list, and hiring and training staff. I began building and honing skills, like customer service and time management. I learned humility and became adept at team leadership, swift problem-solving, and maintaining grace under pressure. I developed and nurtured a real passion for creating great guest experiences.

When I got pregnant with my son, we sold the restaurant and moved to Florida to be close to my parents. My daughter was born three years later. I loved being a mom, but I wanted to get back to work. The world was moving fast; things were changing, and I was feeling left behind.

My ex worked for somebody for a few years but was unhappy, always complaining that they had no idea what they were doing, yet they were opening multiple locations. Instead of looking toward this person as a mentor and learning from their success, he resented it.

Finding a good location was difficult. Whenever a "For Lease" sign appeared at a new construction, it seemed like his employer had insider information and already secured a lease. There was one location we really liked in Coral Springs near my family. We called the landlord the day the sign went up, but it was already claimed by his employer. Several months later we finally found our location and opened our first Florida restaurant in East Boca Raton.

My hands were full raising our young kids during the day and working in the restaurant at night. My ex handled the kitchen while I managed the dining room and service staff. I'd often stay up until 1:00 am or later doing paperwork. Though busy, getting back into the hospitality business reignited my passion.

In an ironic twist, about a month after opening that location, we received a call that the Coral Springs location became available. While my ex complained about people with no restaurant experience opening multiple locations, he was not a risk taker. So when Coral Springs became available, he immediately said no. As I made the call to inform the landlord, my head started spinning and my heart raced; I found myself unexpectedly saying yes. Little did I know that impulsive decision marked the beginning of our successful restaurant enterprise. Although it felt impulsive in the moment, I believed in my vision enough to silence doubts.

Business ventures inherently involve risk. This willingness to embrace risk is a hallmark of many successful entrepreneurs. Not all risks result in success, but without risk, there can be no innovation, growth, or progress. I was willing to bet on myself.

I envisioned neighborhood eateries with superior yet affordable food and service that made guests feel genuinely welcomed. I felt this was lacking in the community. The good restaurants were extremely expensive, and the reasonably priced restaurants were not very good.

Perhaps more important than our customers was our staff. Without a strong team, we had no business at all. This was a point of contention with my ex and something we fought about often. He was old school in an industry notorious for low pay and seven-day work weeks. I believed that if we supported our employees with competitive pay and a work life balance, they would in turn provide excellent care for our customers.

We had a decade of growth and expansion. My skills and knowledge expanded too: business planning, social media, marketing, leadership, sales, networking, and more. I honed the ability to engage positively with challenging and demanding individuals while maintaining a composed demeanor and smile.

During this time, I got divorced. Divorce is never easy. While it started amicably, anger and bitterness led my ex to hire an attorney who turned it into a difficult divorce, adding emotional upheaval to an already full schedule. Several months after the divorce, my ex made the decision to no longer have a relationship with his kids. Essentially, I became a solo parent.

The year was 2008. I owned two restaurants and invested everything I had left in a third. It was an ultra-lounge concept—a little ahead of its time, with an indoor/outdoor bar, fire pit, color changing walls, an incredible sound system, and live music. The restaurant was named LOLA, standing for "Love Often Laugh a Lot," based on an Italian phrase: "Vive Bene Spesso L'amore Di Risata Molto." This was our ethos. There were articles about us in every newspaper and magazine, and we were featured on local TV and news.

The reviews were fabulous. We were busy. The parking lot overflowed. Cars lined up and down the street. Attendance exceeded projections and based on financial projections, we should have been profitable, but broader economic factors impacted us.

The real estate market crashed, and the Bernie Madoff scandal hit my area hard, severely affecting the spending power of many regulars who had invested with him. Average spending was now half of what it was just a year prior. The lease was signed right before the 2008 economic downturn, and the extremely high rent based on pre-crash projections became burdensome overhead. It became increasingly difficult to keep the business afloat.

The younger me may have walked away when confronted with such severe hardship. But I had built grit and unwavering determination, clinging to the mindset that there is a solution to every problem no matter how impossible or insurmountable it seems in the moment. I refused to relinquish control or let external forces write my story.

It is only in the face of adversity that our true strength of character is revealed.

I sold my restaurant in Coral Springs to fund LOLA while looking for an investor. My friend recommended that I speak to his uncle, Shelly. It turns out he was a customer at my restaurants, and he loved them! He agreed to a loan.

Obstacles seemed unending. The most daunting issue uncovered was that we were in arrears with Florida Sales Tax and the IRS. Payments shown as paid had been returned or not processed. My bookkeeper had not accounted for these as she didn't want to add more worry or stress. Burdened as I was, I did not catch this.

I eventually had to close LOLA. The landlord pretended to work with us while searching for another tenant for the location. In the interim, I secured a lease for another location; however, given the circumstances, I decided it was best to put that expansion on hold to stabilize my current situation and concentrate solely on Cucina Mio, my Italian restaurant in Delray.

Though deemed a failure on paper, LOLA was a success. Beneath the financial rubble, it was a marvel in terms of critical acclaim, accolades, customer satisfaction, and personal growth. I emerged stronger, wiser, and more determined, with lessons of grit and perseverance forever changing my character and entrepreneurial blueprint for future ventures.

The closing of LOLA left me with substantial debt, including vendors and the investor loan, for which we had no paperwork, but I resolved to repay it anyway. My Italian restaurant was doing well and allowed me to steadily repay these debts. Shelly, especially, appreciated my efforts to honor our agreement, recognizing that while he did not need repayment, the act itself held significant value.

I went from a net worth in the millions to being in the red. During this period, I made several personal sacrifices, including downsizing my living situation from a large house to a condo. I had children entering college; and they too had expenses that needed to be paid. Remember, I was a solo parent.

Gradually, things began to look up. The lease renewal for my Italian restaurant came up, and I entered negotiations with the landlord for the extension. Meanwhile, the tenant he had secured for the larger LOLA location had already vacated the space, so he wanted me to relocate the Italian restaurant there, but I obviously lacked the capital for such an undertaking. We ultimately did agree on the renewal, which included provisions for me to upgrade the property's exterior among other things.

Acting in good faith based on our agreement, I began making the upgrades then received a letter stating that my lease would not be renewed. I immediately contacted the property manager only to learn that the landlord had decided to lease the larger space to another Italian restaurant. Despite our verbal agreement and the upgrades underway, I found myself without legal recourse.

Doing the right thing came full circle. Shelly was furious with the landlord's dishonorable behavior. I still had the lease for the previously mentioned location, and with Shelly providing half of the financing, I proceeded to open a restaurant there, partnering with others for the rest. The restaurant had a bumpy start with the new partners, for reasons I won't elaborate on, but through persistent hard work, we turned things around, hitting our financial targets.

Things went well for a few years until Shelly passed away. Initially, it was business as usual until the silent partners broke their silence, introducing a new member who questioned our core principles like fair wages and quality ingredients—values and practices that had defined our culture and fueled our success were now suddenly deemed expendable for bottom-line greed.

Moreover, this new partner brought troubling attitudes and prejudice, creating a hostile, toxic atmosphere. It felt like facing daily assault marked by relentless battles and gender discrimination. This intense struggle took a toll on my health and well-being.

It became clear that staying there was no longer viable. So I made the difficult but necessary decision to leave not only that restaurant, but to step back from the restaurant business entirely.

Walking away requires courage. It is scary AF. However, doing so opens space for growth aligned with values.

After over 25 years in the restaurant industry, I found myself at a pivotal fork in the road. I initially started a digital marketing agency, but due to immediate financial needs, I turned my focus to bookkeeping and accounting. This transition not only marked a change in my career but also a step toward a different future as this naturally led to a transition into consulting. My background provided a unique perspective and a deep understanding of the challenges and opportunities in business, and my skillset became an invaluable asset. The digital marketing agency took a back seat as I didn't even have time to work on my own online presence; however, I was not short of satisfied clients or recommendations. Things were moving upward quickly. That was until 2020 when the COVID pandemic struck.

Impacted by the economic downturn caused by the pandemic and with no online presence, as 2020 ended, so did my work with clients. It was during this period of uncertainty that I discovered Clubhouse, an app that became a significant and unexpected influence in my life. This platform, rich with real conversations and knowledge sharing, enabled me to make a profound impact on others. Remarkably, it was through Clubhouse that I met Wendi, Patricia, and Kathy, some of my co-authors for this book. If you had told me that an app would make such a meaningful difference in my life, I would never have believed you, but I assure you, it did.

I spent countless days engaging with people I had never met before, forging connections that led to unexpected collaborations and opened a new avenue for me to share my expertise and experiences. Through our interactions, I rediscovered my passion for mentoring, fueling me to help the next generation of entrepreneurs build thriving ventures.

Inspired by my own journey, I transitioned to become a business growth strategist and trusted advisor with a unique combination of financial expertise, operational insights, and firsthand entrepreneurial experience. Instead of Clubhouse I now share my knowledge and insights on LinkedIn, which has led to the honor of being named a LinkedIn top voice. This new journey has only just begun.

What unique framework or service do you offer to your community or clients?

I leverage my background as a CPA combined with 25+ years in hospitality leadership and entrepreneurship to equip and empower seasoned professionals and subject matter experts to turn their expertise into a thriving, profitable venture. Whether looking to start a new business or grow an existing one, together we navigate the complexities of the business landscape. I offer both group coaching to facilitate peer knowledge sharing and targeted one-on-one consulting with personalized strategies and mentorship in business development, marketing, branding, and financial management.

My own journey continues to evolve, fueled by a deep commitment to making a difference and creating a legacy by helping others achieve sustainable success.

What life or business lessons have created the most growth for you?

It is by facing and overcoming major hardships that we uncover the full extent of our resilience, determination, and ability to persevere. The commitment to doing the right thing, even when it's hard or not convenient, is the true mark of leadership, character, and the individual strength that can inspire others. I was 45 years old when I first went through the type of struggle that defines strength of character, but it was the paths chosen and lessons learned along the way that forged the steel.

What is your ultimate impact?

Entrepreneurship often starts with a dream—a vision to build something meaningful to leave as a legacy. I have the privilege of equipping clients with the tools and knowledge for financial and professional success, thus empowering them to provide services that contribute positively to others' success and well-being, thereby fostering a cycle of prosperity and positive change. That is my ultimate impact.

How can people connect with you?

I can be found at ShoreAdvice.Com and at WendyShore.co

IF YOU STILL NEED TO FIGURE OUT YOUR PURPOSE, LISTEN TO THOSE WHO BELIEVE IN YOU AND RECOGNIZE THE POTENTIAL FOR IMPACT.

Amber Stitt

CHAPTER 13

EMPOWERING OTHERS IN THE FACE OF ADVERSITY BY AMBER STITT

The glare of the blinding stage lights made it difficult to put on my microphone, especially in my sleeveless one-piece dress. I had intentionally chosen something comfortable but also business professional, not expecting to be on the main stage. My initial plan was to participate in a breakout session, discussing ways to have a successful virtual business among my peers. However, the production team unexpectedly miked me up and thrust me into the spotlight on the main stage without a moment's notice. In the backdrop, it was 2019, right on the edge of the impending COVID-19 pandemic. We were in Las Vegas, and the city and casino floors felt oddly quiet and deserted, starkly contrasting to its usual bustling atmosphere. Little did I know this would turn out to be one of the final conferences before the world as we knew it and our everyday routines suddenly ground to a halt in 2020.

I had become a mother just three months ago, and my strategy for the conference was a delicate balancing act between attending presentations and catching up with colleagues, all while sneaking back to my hotel room to pump milk for my four-month-old baby at home. Given my four-hour sleep segments with my daughter, my preparations were necessarily minimal for this event. I was encouraged to present on building a virtual business, a subject I was immersed in for the past five years. However, the audience needed to know that I recently concluded a two-year noncompete agreement, and my practice was being rebuilt from the ground up. I was a new parent and was essentially starting from scratch as a new business owner, although I already had five years of experience in my industry. Despite my hesitations and insecurities, I found myself thrust onto the main stage under the unforgiving spotlight. It was an opportunity, right? Why not?

The dress I had chosen, while concealing my post-pregnancy figure, restricted my movement, making it difficult to navigate the stage confidently. The shoes didn't help either, as they prevented me from walking comfortably on the main stage floorboards. They were more shifty and flexible than they looked from the audience. Though well-intentioned, the encouragement from my peers added to my anxiety, especially since I hadn't had the opportunity to practice my presentation properly and wanted to do a good job for them. I hastily put together some PowerPoint slides and found myself standing on that stage, blinking into the bright lights, and forgetting to switch my slides while speaking. I also was trying to play it cool by leaning next to the podium to steady myself. I am not sure how cool it looked, especially after my colleague whispered from the audience that I hadn't clicked forward to share my slides with everyone. (Thanks, Bob!) I imagine my face was flushed once I learned about that. I laughed it off and tried to make fun of it while speaking and carried on.

Despite the mishaps, I managed to talk for a full 45 minutes, though it felt more like a casual conversation with the audience. I walked off the stage with mixed feelings—a sense of accomplishment for taking the leap and an unrelenting feeling that I could have done better.

This experience marked the beginning of a transformative journey in my life. It was a time when people believed in me and my message, even if I didn't fully believe in myself. They saw something unique in my work and pushed me to share it with a broader audience. It was challenging, but it ignited a desire to improve and connect with others.

My self-doubt was trying to creep in post-presentation with nagging thoughts as I joined my peers in the audience that day. Those pessimistic thoughts came home with me back to Arizona, trying to push me to dwell on past performance. But strangely, another voice within me emerged, urging me to move forward and not let the negativity hold me back. When I finally listened and shut out the gloomy self-talk, it was fascinating how life began to change.

After that point, I took it upon myself to explore the world of public speaking, and I've pursued numerous opportunities since then. I told myself that was my first attempt, and it could only get better from here. While I'm still a work in progress today, the nerves are still there, but I've gained the confidence to deliver my message with conviction. All this because I refused to surrender to the emotions that once held me back.

As we navigate different phases of life, there are moments when we feel like we're starting over, questioning our knowledge and purpose. However, these moments can be an opportunity to inspire and impact others with our stories.

What is the "why" behind what you do?

At the tender age of 10, my family was thrust into an unimaginable tragedy. I vividly remember that late August day, just after my father's birthday. We eagerly anticipated visiting our local pool because Midwestern summers provide only a few opportunities for pool enjoyment. My mother was dressed in a blue-green sundress and had just picked my brother and I up (two of the four children) from school. I remember her standing by the car while waiting for us, dress flowing in the breeze. She was excited to see us. We were all set to head home, change into bathing suits, and make the most of the afternoon.

However, our plans took a drastic turn when my mother's friend unexpectedly entered our kitchen through the garage door entryway. It was unusual because she usually doesn't join us on such outings. Even though I was the oldest among my siblings, I couldn't help but eavesdrop on their conversation. I strained to make sense of what was being said, but all I could make out were eventually distressed screams from my mother. It was as if the world around me shifted, and I found myself in a fog of shock for what felt like an eternity. I actually still can't remember how I learned that my two-year old brother had passed away that day, but I do remember just slumping to the kitchen floor in disbelief and shock took over.

My late brother was vacationing with my grandparents in Sarasota, Florida with my then five-year old sister. He was supposed to be napping, but he must have climbed out of bed and went out to the pool through one of the bathroom entrances to the pool deck. We speculated that he was being a curious toddler, heading out to the pool deck alone to explore. We don't have final details of the exact how and when he passed away that afternoon, but he did try to swim alone that day. My grandparents made the call to my father, and he must have sent my mom's friend to our house to break the news.

In those following two weeks, our home became a revolving door of visitors, with well-wishers bringing food and flowers. I, on the other hand, sat in a daze as people moved around me. When the funeral came, I couldn't bring myself to look at my brother in the open casket, fearing that it would be the only memory I'd have of him. I felt I had my closure because he wasn't here anymore in my home.

As time passed, I could hear my father's sorrowful sobs echoing down the hallway in the evenings, as he mourned the loss of his young son. Brief memories came and went, but much of that period remains a haze for me and still does. My little brother had often been my responsibility as the eldest, and my mother had placed her trust in me to look after him, which made the loss even more heartbreaking because we were so close.

Looking back on those challenging days and the years that came after, I can now see how this tragedy has deeply shaped my journey as an adult, spouse, parent, business owner, and now a financial consultant. I've personally witnessed the impact on a family when they're unprepared for unexpected hardships. My father, an entrepreneur with now three children instead of four, had to navigate life's complexities while maintaining a business as he was the sole provider. Even though he had some plans to prepare for the unthinkable, it took a while for my father and mother to be able to face the day.

During times of unforeseen hardship, whether it's the loss of a loved one or a debilitating illness, there's a period when it feels like you're standing still, unable to take action. The mind instinctively goes into survival mode, trying to shield you from the harsh reality. In these moments, I've found my purpose—helping families plan effectively for life's challenges so they can regain control and navigate life with resilience.

Without adequate planning for life's unpredictable twists and turns, there's a risk that you will suffer and fall under chronic stress, but those around you will also suffer due to the absence of a well-thought-out plan. My life's mission is to ensure that others are well-prepared to face the unexpected, empowering them to manage life's trials with strength and determination.

What life lessons have created the most growth for you?

My journey into business ownership kicked off during a pivotal moment in my life. Six months into my pregnancy, I took the plunge and left my job to launch my own venture. Previously, I worked as a part of my family's business, and I truly appreciated the opportunities they provided me. However, I clearly envisioned a specific niche that resonated with me. Uncertain about the demands of motherhood and needing the flexibility to manage my new role as a parent, I realized that starting my own company was the only way to fine-tune that niche and build the systems necessary to embrace motherhood and my passion for making a difference in people's lives.

I also realized that many of us tend to downplay our expertise and hide our talents out of fear that we will come off as arrogant if we show off our abilities to others. I have learned through my professional community to embrace the opportunity to shine. It became evident that as individuals we all have a purpose and a voice that can make a difference in the lives of others. We all do!

If you still need to figure out your purpose, listen to those who believe in you and recognize the potential for impact. Your superpowers—what people see in you that you might not see—are revealed when you hear someone encouraging you through words, introductions to others, or compliments on a job well done. Don't overlook these statements, responding with a statement such as "Oh, you are just being nice," as this could be the key to figuring out your purpose.

I encourage anyone with a new idea or a calling to treat it seriously, as it could be the start of something meaningful. Elizabeth Gilbert would agree with me as well. In her book *Big Magic* she says, "The universe buries strange jewels deep within us all, and then stands back to see if we can find them." Surrounding oneself with like-minded individuals who support these ideas and understand your vision is crucial. It's essential to move beyond environments that don't align with your goals and believe in your unique ability to make a difference.

During the pandemic, I developed a five-step process called the "Pathways of Peak Performance," aimed at building resilience in one's business and personal life. While it may not have initially made sense in the insurance industry I worked within, it resonated with individuals seeking a better life, and it can lay the groundwork for your business. This experience taught me that stepping out of your comfort zone and exploring new avenues is okay if it aligns with your passion and purpose.

I've also realized that once you are pursuing your passion, you don't have to confine yourself to a single path if you don't want to. Find your niche, leverage your talents, and allow other business opportunities to evolve naturally. Collaborate with a supportive community, delegate tasks, and harness the strengths of those around you to bring your vision to life.

In the journey of personal development, discipline, consistency, and meditation are common themes among successful individuals. Cultivating these practices can propel your entrepreneurial endeavors and help you embrace the belief that you have something valuable to share with the world.

Opportunities often arise when you least expect them and remaining open-minded and motivated is crucial. Seek out a community that aligns with your mission and values and don't be swayed by those who don't understand your vision. Again, surround yourself with people who inspire you and share your drive to make an impact. I cannot stress how important this is to the implementation of your ideas.

In today's world, communication with others is the currency that transcends time and technology. Whether through storytelling, podcasts, or other forms, working on your ongoing message may have a profound impact wherever you go. Embrace the idea that your voice, your ideas, and your stories have the power to change lives.

What role do collaboration and community have in your business?

After my experience back in 2019, I took it upon myself to explore the world of public speaking. I've pursued numerous opportunities to speak out and work with nonprofits since then, focusing on thought leadership and bringing people to financial freedom. While I'm still a work in progress—the nerves are still there—I've gained the confidence to deliver my message with conviction. All this because I refused to surrender to the negativity that once held me back. I have channeled this energy and focus into my podcast, and I interview people from all walks of life. Having conversations with others to bring thought leadership to all has been so helpful to my community and to me. There are so many ways now to find your tribe either online or virtually. I find this critical for those who are just starting out in business or going through a transition. We all can benefit from mentorship and menteeship. Paulo Coelho once said, "The Power of storytelling is exactly this: to bridge the gaps where everything else has crumbled." I take this to mean that our stories are the most effective way of communicating with others. This is where we can genuinely make a difference in the lives of others and in our own lives.

What is your ultimate impact?

Having experienced a profound loss at a young age, I gained firsthand insight into the emotional and practical hurdles that families confront in challenging times. This experience has instilled in me a deep well of empathy and compassion, igniting my passion to alleviate the suffering of others.

Resilience isn't just a trendy word in my vocabulary. I first encountered it during a workshop a few years back, and it struck me as a beautiful, gentle term that encapsulates our ability to embrace tragedy and absorb its impact. Then, like a phoenix rising from the ashes, you can emerge stronger and purpose-driven: transformed.

Inherently motivated by a sense of duty and inspired by my family's ability to endure tough times, I've developed a system to help guide others. Harnessing my own strengths and the ability to overcome the darkest moments, I aim to empower others to do the same and positively impact those around them. This resilience is a constant source of inspiration, guiding my mission to empower others to tackle their challenges with determination.

Reflecting on the events of 1990 and even in 2020, I've understood the profound impact of unpreparedness. I observed how shock and stress can disrupt one's work and mental clarity, compelling one into a survival mode. Witnessing my family's struggle to navigate life after our tragedy underscores the significance of planning for unforeseen contingencies.

This unique perspective has shaped my approach to gently guide my clients in proactive planning without inducing fear. I firmly advocate for taking action today to initiate planning, recognizing that everyone has a different journey when it comes to setting financial goals and safeguarding their families. I'm determined to make a difference by helping others prepare effectively for life's uncertainties, and encouraging them to take action while they are well and able.

My brother's story has been shared countless times by my father, who offers pro bono speaking and counseling to those who have faced similar challenges in his community. I, too, share this story with care when the time is right, urging individuals to consider their loved ones and what would happen to them in the face of adversity. Have we organized our lives and minds to address unfortunate circumstances?

Ultimately, my story is about empowerment. It expresses my commitment to empower individuals and families to seize control of their lives by proactively addressing potential hurdles, equipping them with the knowledge and tools to face the unexpected with confidence and resilience. My ultimate mission is to assist individuals and families in regaining control of their lives during challenging times.

Now, returning to entrepreneurship, what are you called to help others with? This is your moment to determine the solutions you offer and bring them into the world.

My primary impact can be summarized within the "Pathways of Peak Performance," a five-step process I've developed to steer individuals toward success and fulfillment.

1. **Focusing on Talents and Doing What You Love:** I'm a firm believer that recognizing your individual talents and interests is the initial stride toward both personal and professional

contentment. When you align your calling with your innate skills and genuine passions, not only do you experience heightened satisfaction but you also unleash your full potential for achieving greatness. My mission is to motivate others to unearth their talents and follow their genuine passions. When you're clear on these aspects, they can serve as a guiding light, a beacon in the midst of uncertainty.

2. **Focusing on Money Goals and Financial Freedom:** Being financially free is a fundamental aspect of a fulfilling life and having security. Through financial education and goal-setting, I aim to empower individuals to take control of their financial futures, based on their talents and personality type. This involves understanding their financial goals, managing resources wisely, and working toward financial freedom to enjoy life without unnecessary financial stress.

3. **Transferring Risk to Handle Obstacles:** Life is full of uncertainties and challenges. To thrive in both the personal and business realms, it's crucial to manage and mitigate risks effectively. My approach emphasizes the importance of organization, risk management, and insurance to protect against unforeseen obstacles. This allows individuals to navigate life's ups and downs with greater confidence.

4. **Innovating with Marketing and Technologies:** In the rapidly evolving landscape of today's world, keeping up with the latest marketing strategies and emerging technologies is paramount for achieving success. I urge individuals to welcome innovation, be flexible in response to shifting trends, and harness the potential of technology to elevate both their professional endeavors and personal experiences. It's crucial to fully embrace the technology at our disposal while concurrently refining our personal branding, digital presence, and engagement with our communities.

5. **Building a Community of Common Minds:** Success is a collective endeavor. Creating a supportive community of

like-minded individuals who share common goals and values is essential. This network can offer mentorship, guidance, and the opportunity for valuable partnerships. By collaborating, we can combine our strengths, inspire one another, and push toward greater achievements. Sometimes, you'll discover this support may actually extend beyond your immediate family and close friends. It's important to be mindful of those who might be envious or unsupportive and those who don't reciprocate the same positive energy you bring into their lives.

My ultimate impact revolves around helping individuals discover their talents, achieve financial freedom, manage risks effectively, embrace innovation, and build a supportive community. By following the framework of the "Pathways of Peak Performance," I aim to inspire and empower others to lead fulfilling lives, both personally and professionally, while positively impacting their communities and the world at large.

How can people connect with you?

I can be found at AmberStitt.com and on Instagram @AmberStitt_

BEFORE YOU CAN GROW A BUSINESS, YOU MUST GROW YOURSELF.

Daniela Thelusma

CHAPTER 14

THE UNBROKEN KODE: UNLEASHING THE SUCCESS IN YOUR VEINS BY DANIELA THELUSMA

"I want to be with you," I hear myself saying.

"I know," says my mother over the phone. "I want to be with you, too. Don't worry. Everything will be fine."

I'm only three years old, but I can tell just by the sound of my mother's voice that she's been crying. Many people say they have trouble accessing childhood memories from before they were three or four years old, but for me, this memory is as vivid in my mind as the day it happened. In fact, it's my *very first* memory: my foster mother handing me the phone and telling me that my mom, my *real* mom, was on the line.

I think this was the first moment I truly understood that I wasn't with my mother. I was somewhere, and she was somewhere else. I was going to be there, away from her, for an unknown amount of time. It also was the moment when I realized something was going on that I just didn't quite understand. I knew I had a mother, but she wasn't here. Instead, I was with a foster mother, a woman I didn't really know yet. Why was this happening?

"I want to be with you," little three-year-old Daniela tells her mother over the phone, again. It's too hard to articulate the more complicated feelings.

"And you know I want to be with you too, *kode*," she says, calling me by her nickname for me, a Cape Verdean term of endearment for the youngest child of the family. "Everything will be fine. I'm going to come get you soon. I promise."

I couldn't have known it at the time, but my mother was in the grips of mental illness that she had been fighting for years even back in Cape Verde (an archipelago off the west coast of Africa) and lost custody of me as a result of the untreated condition. To say that this twist of fate was heartbreaking for my mother doesn't do justice to the pain she went through. Ask anyone who has ever had their kids taken away or knows someone who has been through this, and they'll tell you how devastating it is and how difficult it is to get your child back again. Especially when you are an immigrant, new to the country, and don't speak English. It's a truly gruesome process, and it can wear you down and break you if you're not strong enough.

At the age of three, I was placed in a foster home, separated from my family. Thank God I had a phenomenal foster mother who treated me well. I actually have some very good memories from that time. Yet, always in the back of my mind I felt that I wasn't supposed to be there, and I felt out of place. I wanted to be with my mother.

Thankfully, things didn't go too far. I wasn't adopted into the system, but I was held in foster care for a certain amount of time. My mother was able to get treatment and work with a fantastic case manager who advocated for her. She walked my mother through the proper procedures and helped her get realigned, situated, and back on her feet. With her help, my mother was able to get me back, and my family was finally reunited.

The power of a mother's love

Life after that was great. Up until that point, I had no memory of my siblings, so finally getting to meet them was one of the most impactful moments of my childhood. And having my mother back meant more to me than I could express or probably even fully comprehend at the time.

What I remember about our home was that there was so much love there. And although times were tough, I was being raised by the best woman in the world. God was a major part of our home life, and prayer was a priority. My mother taught us that whenever we prayed, we were to kneel down properly and speak to God to thank him for our blessings. It was there that my faith took root—faith in God and faith that everything would be fine, as long as we took care of one another. After all, that's what my mother had told me over the phone. "Everything will be fine. I'm going to come get you soon, I promise." And she kept that promise.

My mother gave us literally every single thing she had. She struggled to provide, and yet somehow, not once did we go without food or shelter. I'll never forget the day when the fridge was *empty*. All we had left were a few eggs, only enough for each of us, my mother, my sister, and I. Even now, I can picture the scene: us sitting there with our egg. We put salt on it and we began to eat. But then, my mother took her egg, looked at it, and instead of eating it, split it in half. Without saying anything, she handed one half to me and the other to my sister. Both of us started crying. It pained me to know that she was going to go hungry just so we could have a little more.

"Mommy, we can't eat this," I remember my sister saying. "You literally haven't eaten all day."

"Take ours!" we pleaded with her through our tears, trying to hand it back to her. "Just please, take it back!"

"No, no," she said calmly. "You both eat."

Kode (pronounced KO-dé) is a word that continues to be important to me to this day.

I'm sure this wasn't the only time my mother went without eating so we could eat. A mother's love is powerful, especially when you see it in action. Even when my mother was hanging by a thread, she spoke life into us. She constantly told my sister and I that we would grow up to be great women or in our language "grande mujer." She was exhausted, overworked, and overwhelmed doing it all alone. Despite it all, she was able to get her driver's license, work multiple jobs at once, and still maintain her household the best that she could. I couldn't have known it at the time, but all this was setting me up to one day discover, and eventually achieve, my ultimate impact.

Success is in your veins: A life lesson that created growth for me

At 14 years old I started working my first job at a summer program through my high school. My sister and I both started working around that age out of a desire to help our mother. It started with summer jobs. And after that, we were able to get our workers' permits and work after school on the weekdays.

My first job was at a Subway sandwich shop. By then, my sister had a child of her own to look after, my niece. So when my first ever paycheck came in, I decided to give it to her.

"I can't accept this," she said at first.

"No, no, you take it," I told her. "I want you to do whatever you need to do with this."

It's amazing, in hindsight, how this event echoes the story of my mother giving us her last egg. But it's just how we were raised. That's what you do for your family. You take care of one another.

I worked at Subway for close to seven years and was lucky enough to have just about the best boss anyone could have asked for. He and his wife became early mentors for me. He was an entrepreneur, and she was a nurse who was always working overtime. The more I got to know her, the more she inspired me, and the more interested I became in her line of work.

I don't know what it was—maybe it came from seeing my mother making so many sacrifices for her kids or maybe it was an innate work ethic passed down from my family—but I had a strong drive within me. I think this is something God must have instilled in me because it came quite naturally. I was always self-propelled and willing to go the extra mile.

I was almost always working multiple jobs. By the time I was 15 or 16, I had become *that* friend, the one who everybody knows won't be able to make it. "She's probably *working* again." Everyone else had all this extra time to go out on the weekends, go to the movies, hang out, and just enjoy their youth. By the time I was 18, I was also working at a nursing home (more on that later), in addition to my other part-time jobs. Of course, you can't keep going at that sort of pace forever. Eventually, it starts to take its toll.

A pivotal moment for me came in the summer when I was working the opening shift at Subway, then driving all the way out to the neighboring town to work until 11:00 pm at the nursing home. I remember driving in the car and calling my mom after work. My back was killing me and my feet hurt so badly that it felt like they were burning. This was the result of being severely understaffed and overworked. But mostly, I was just exhausted.

"Mom," I said, "I'm just... so tired."

I didn't know what else to say anymore. I felt like I was about to break.

"Just come home and rest, kode," she told me. "It's fine. You don't have to work this much!"

The truth was, I was using her car, and I was trying to save up to get a vehicle of my own. I knew my future depended on it. So I did have to work that hard. My mother financially couldn't help me, and I didn't have anyone else that I could count on to help me.

After I hung up, I remember just crying. The work ethic, the drive, was in me. But at the same time, I couldn't help but wonder, why? Why was this so hard? I'm so young! My back shouldn't hurt like this! I shouldn't be this tired!

And then, it was like I heard my mother over the phone line again: *Everything will be fine.*

It was as if, all at once, I realized, "This too shall pass." Everything really was going to be fine. Thanks to God and my mother and the story of all I'd been through, everything I needed, all the answers, were already within me. I just had to believe.

At that moment, five words came to me: Success is in your veins.

All my successes were waiting within me. I just had to believe and trust that voice coming from inside.

Was that night hard? Yes. Was I still tired and in pain? You better believe it! But those words gave me newfound stamina. Success is in your veins.

I remained unbroken. I put my foot on the gas pedal and kept going.

What is the "why" behind what you do?

When it came to entrepreneurship, I knew the term. I knew that certain people were entrepreneurs. I even got to see my boss at Subway and his wife living that dream, but the idea of owning and operating a business took a while to grow within me. The first stirrings were when I felt the urge to one day open my own wellness center.

My passion for the wellness field came early on, from seeing my mother fight through her illness. When you're a first-generation child of immigrants, you sort of become the default translator for the rest of your family members, so my sister and I often went with my mother to her appointments. Helping my mother navigate her medical journey was my first introduction to healthcare and the field of nursing.

I became further drawn to the medical field through the example of my boss's wife, who worked as a nurse and was passionate about providing care to her patients. So when I found out that Brockton High School offered a program where students could earn their CNA (Certified Nursing Assistant) certification while they were still enrolled in high school, I jumped at the chance.

I'm not sure how many people can say they earned their CNA in high school while still working after school, but that's exactly what I did! I tried to take as many hours as I possibly could at work, often getting close to a full-time schedule while still in high school, and I kept saving up my money. I knew I would need a car of my own if I wanted to get into a clinical setting when I got into college. Thankfully, taking my CNA certification exam through my high school meant I didn't have to pay the usual fee to take the test, which helped make it possible for me to get my certification.

After that I graduated, I passed my CNA exam, and went to Regis College in Massachusetts. I had a clinical at Boston Children's Hospital that inspired me to want to work there. It felt like my dream job. I felt there was still a part of me that liked the idea of one day owning and running my own clinic.

After college, I went on to get my master's degree in nursing leadership administration and then as a family nurse practitioner. While finishing my second master's degree, I also worked as a nurse at Boston Health Care for the Homeless (BHCHP), a nonprofit that provides healthcare for homeless individuals in the Greater Boston Area. What's unique about this program is that it's a combination shelter and medical clinic, where struggling individuals can get the help they need.

This new experience really resonated with me. It not only solidified my desire to work in a clinic setting, but it reminded me of my goal to own and operate a clinic of my own. God had planted the seed of that idea in me, and now I felt compelled to pursue it. It was the greatest way I felt I could help others.

I now knew this was my "why," the ultimate impact I was meant to bring to the world.

What advice would you give to someone considering entrepreneurship?

My husband and I were able to achieve our dream of building a wellness center together, but being an entrepreneur isn't easy. So if I were to give one piece of advice to someone considering entrepreneurship, it would be to practice delayed gratification.

In a microwave generation, I would argue that we're so used to getting things fast—we're used to getting them instantly! But that's not how being an entrepreneur works. You've got to play the long game, whether that means working two jobs to save up for a car or if you're a parent, depriving yourself of the last egg, just so your kids don't go hungry.

And don't forget: Before you can grow a business, you must grow yourself. Get uncomfortable. Read books outside your field. Hone your skill set. And choose the company you keep wisely; make sure the people you're surrounded by are good influences. I think that's one way that God has always blessed me, even from an early age.

If you take nothing else away from this chapter, I hope you've at least seen how powerful an individual's personal story can be. Many of us try to escape from our past. I urge you to own it. Don't just accept your story, love it. Take the time to reflect on where you are now and where you've been. It's not easy to open up, get vulnerable, and share your personal history (especially when some parts aren't pretty). But your story could be a source of great strength and inspiration to millions.

Sometimes, we can be so critical of ourselves that it causes roadblocks on the path toward achieving our ultimate impact as entrepreneurs. Remember who you are. Embrace your story and if you're going to fall, fall forward and be compassionate enough to extend the same grace to yourself that you give to others.

And finally, give your dream to God. Have the faith that He will align your path.

I hope it's clear by now that without my mother, there is no story here. Without her, there is no me. The things she went through could have broken her, but a mother's love empowered her to persevere through it all. And it continues to do so for me to this day.

I've never stopped being her unbroken kode.

What is your ultimate impact?

Fast-forward to today, and I almost can't believe where I'm at. It's like, "Pinch me, I must be dreaming." With my husband, Steve, I was able to co-found LivLux Wellness, a health and wellness clinic where we take the motto of "success is in your veins" literally.

At LivLux, we focus a lot on proactive care and maintenance— wellness care instead of disease care. Some of the most helpful services we offer are biomarker testing, intravenous hydration, and vitamin replacement therapy. It's common knowledge that many people are vitamin deficient. Here, you can see in an instant exactly which vitamins and minerals you're deficient in through a six-month snapshot.

At a glance, our team can see

- The state of your immune system
- How your body is reacting to the foods you're eating
- Vitamin levels
- Mineral levels
- Chemical analysis
- Environmental tests, mold, and more

Another example of a service we offer is IV hydration. A lot of people get IV hydration when they're sick, and there's nothing wrong with that. But why not have that as a preventative measure instead of as a last resort? You can get the hydration, vitamins, and minerals into your body before your body is in distress.

I love that all of this is so accessible. The problem is most people don't even know services like this are available, which is why part of our health and wellness mission is educating people. Health care is much less expensive when you pay for it when you're well instead of when you're ill.

LivLux Wellness is everything we ever envisioned it to be and more, and I feel honored and privileged to be on this journey. In a way, I can't believe how far I've come, but at the same time, the mission dream hasn't changed. My job is still to take care of people and to see them experience wellness and well-being and wholeness and vitality.

My ultimate impact comes back to the way I grew up and what I desired for my own family. All I want is for people to feel secure. I want them to feel that they are in great hands.

Whether you call them patients or clients or family, the mission doesn't change.

How can people connect with you?

I can be found at livluxwellness.com and on Instagram @fndani

IF YOU WANT LOVE,
GIVE IT FIRST. IF YOU
WANT A CONNECTION,
CONNECT FIRST.

Steve Thelusma

CHAPTER 15

THE IMPACT-DRIVEN FAITH-PRENEUR: BELIEVING IN THE UNSEEN BY STEVE THELUSMA

At first glance, life can appear to be full of coincidences. You take a step in one direction and happen to meet exactly the right person at exactly the right time. You think of an old high school friend, and the next day they call you on the phone. Personally, I don't believe in coincidences and never have because coincidences are just God's way of remaining anonymous.

Each one of us begins life with a finite viewpoint; the scope of our view is limited by the circumstances around us. Growing up in Haiti, all I knew was my own situation. Our country was beautiful, and contrary to what you see on the news, it was peaceful. When I think of Haiti, I think of its serenity.

That's not to say things were perfect. In my childhood home, we had electricity only occasionally. It would come on once in a while (if we were lucky enough to happen to be in the part of the city where the power grid was turned on). I can still remember the smell of the burning charcoal that we used to cook our meals. Unless a hard rain had provided us with some fresh water, each day, my brother and I would walk a mile or two to the local well to fetch water and bring it back to the house, sometimes in gallon-size jugs and other times in a bucket. Go down the hill, draw the water, haul it back up to the house, and repeat.

My first introduction to entrepreneurship came from my mother and father. My mother had her own boutique, where she sold clothes and sneakers, and my dad, when he wasn't working his day job for the water company, was always baking and cooking and selling his culinary products. These days, we call those sorts of things "side hustles." Back then, we called it surviving and providing.

Looking back on it now, one of the things I'm most grateful for was that I got to see the entrepreneurial journey in action through my parents. Even in the best of circumstances, it's not easy to build a business, let alone in the sort of situation we were in. I admired my mother's drive and determination in particular. It wasn't just her work ethic that inspired me; it was the courage that she had to even consider being an entrepreneur.

God hears me, and the journey begins

When I was a child, everyone in Haiti spoke about America like it was the Promised Land. Although I appreciated the home I had and knew that my mother and father were doing their best, I always felt like there was something bigger out there. Deep down, I knew there was more out there waiting for me. I didn't know what that would look like, but I knew there had to be some other avenue I could take.

I'll never forget the day this vague feeling shifted into stark focus for me. I was just a young boy at the time. I was sitting on some rocks, talking with one of my best friends after we had just finished playing sports outside. It wasn't an uncommon occurrence. But that day, the conversation got deeper than usual.

"Hey," I said, "this can't be life, can it?"

"What do you mean?" he asked.

"I mean, I know my mother and father are working hard in Haiti. I see my aunt working three jobs. I see my uncle working two or three jobs. And... I don't want to do that when I'm older."

That was when it hit me. *This cannot be how life is supposed to be. I refuse to accept it.* At that moment, I made the conscious decision that even though I didn't know what life was supposed to be like or even what I was supposed to do, I would have faith. I believed that God would show me. He would reveal it to me, and with His help I was going to go out into the world and make my way.

Like I said, I've never believed in coincidences, and it was no coincidence that such a thought came into my head.

Once I put that desire out into the universe, God heard me, and the wheels started turning.

As I said, our viewpoint is limited by our circumstances. You can only know as far as you can *see*. But once your mind's been opened and expanded, it can never retract again.

When it came to everything my family had done for me, I was thankful. They did what they had to do in order to provide for me. But their destiny wasn't my own. There had to be more.

To put it simply, my entrepreneurial journey was never a question of dollars. It was never a financial goal. It was always a freedom goal. As a Purple Heart veteran, I was fighting for freedom but always felt that I never had any. I wanted to live the sort of life that my hard-working parents deserved but never had. I knew I couldn't do it all on my own, but I had the faith to know I didn't have to do it on my own.

What is the "why" behind what you do?

At this point, I had decided once and for all that I wanted to be an entrepreneur. Everything in my life so far seemed like it had been leading me to this. But it's easier said than done, right? In fact, there was a period of time shortly after when I really decided that I wanted to be an entrepreneur. I wanted to go build businesses and help people and in turn help my family be financially free. This was when I was ridiculed for my dream. I got made fun of for having a vision that no one could see. They were actually *laughing* at me when I told them about it. Everyone thought it was a joke because nobody in my family had ever seen a millionaire before, especially at my age. In their minds, I should have been content with having a job, working a 9–5 (which isn't an issue), but I could see something greater for myself.

After leaving my sales development role at a firm in Boston, I found myself in a sales and marketing role. Then when I walked away from that, that's when I moved down to Florida, where my wife Daniela and I dipped our toes into real estate. We had always talked about getting into health, nutrition, and wellness because of our passion for helping others. So after cashing out on a large property deal, we took the profit and invested in LivLux Wellness, Inc., a health and wellness business.

Our experience with LivLux Wellness has brought me to an important conclusion about my work: the why behind everything I do is to help people become better versions of themselves from the inside out. That's the foundation behind my identity as a faith-preneur.

I've said it before, and I'll say it again:

There's no such thing as coincidences.

Being a faith-preneur means not only having immovable faith in God, but also unshakable faith in yourself. It fires me up to share this with you now because that's how my faith works. Over time, I've learned that while faith without works is dead, the only thing that you really need is undeniable belief because God will take care of the rest.

When everyone else thought my vision was a joke, that was when I had to dig deep. If I hadn't been able to find that faith within myself when everyone was laughing, to believe in myself when nobody else did, all my entrepreneurial failures that eventually led to success would never have happened.

In that way, my why goes beyond just helping others through our business. It's encouraging others to have the sort of faith that's required to reach their dreams.

What life or business lessons have created the most growth for you?

Fortunately, school came easy for me. I loved learning, and I was always reading. More importantly, I was observant of the world around me. My parents' goal for their children was a better life. And as much as it must have hurt them to send me to America, it was a sacrifice they were willing to make if it meant they could give their children a better chance at life.

I made the move to the US when I was nine years old. I continued to do well in school there, but I was always working or playing football. Eventually, I stopped playing football because I was working so much and sending part of every paycheck home to my parents. For a while, I lived in Boston. By the time I was 17, I had moved to Port St. Lucie, Florida, and I was working more than ever to figure out the next chapter of my life.

At that time, my siblings and I worked hard to send money to our mother, who was a survivor of a serious stroke that changed her life. Her entrepreneurial journey came to an abrupt end. That said, I still had to fend for myself in the US to an extent, between transportation, food, and all the little bills that accumulated. These are the sorts of things a lot of kids don't have to worry about during their senior year of high school.

At Centennial High School, I participated in the Navy Junior Reserve Officers Training Corps (NJROTC) program. I loved the atmosphere, the discipline, and the organizational structure. I saw it as the sort of environment where I could thrive and succeed. So after graduating from Centennial High School, I enlisted in the United States Navy Seabees.

During my six years in the Navy, I did deployments to Afghanistan and spent some time in Iraq. I worked disaster relief in Japan for almost a year when the tsunami hit. I initially went into the military with the plan of staying in for 20 years, but during my last tour, I was involved in multiple incidents that eventually led to me being awarded a Purple Heart medal. My decision to leave the Navy after that had less to do with what occurred on the battlefield and more to do with the fact that the Navy was no longer taking me where I wanted to go. I realized that there was more in me, and it was time to move on.

So, how did this lead me to becoming an entrepreneur? Well, it all comes back to putting it in God's hands and letting Him figure out how.

I started working with a network marketing company during my time in the Navy and ended up going to a lot of events to develop myself, reading a lot about personal growth, and trying to take the next step in my journey. I knew I had always been great in sales and marketing and speaking and just generally being in the front of the room.

At one point, I held a few quality jobs in between, enough to whet my appetite and learn valuable lessons. You see, I'm a numbers guy, and what I saw in those jobs really put things into perspective for me. The process went something like this. As the salesperson, I would put in the time, the energy—basically all the work—to sell a $20,000, $40,000, or maybe even a $70,000 product. I initiated the customer interaction and saw it through from start to finish. I was the one showing off the product, communicating with the customer, and bringing the client to the closing table. This so I could get between 5 percent and 8 percent of the total deal. And, to be clear, we're not talking about the total cost; we're talking about just a percent of the profit margin. That's a percentage of the profit made on the deal.

The entire structure just didn't make sense to me. It is no coincidence that I worked those positions for a limited time. I was just a grunt on the front lines, working my butt off to make money for somebody else, but I could picture myself owning those businesses, running things, being the one in charge of the place instead of the one doing all the grunt work. At that time, I certainly didn't have the capital required to make something like that happen. So the next step was clear: figure out the capital side of the equation.

What role do collaboration and community have in your business?

My entire childhood, I saw my parents working hard to provide for us, making every sacrifice, even a sacrifice as painful as sending us thousands of miles away to give us the blessing of a chance to thrive in this life. To honor that legacy, I didn't just want to be successful. I wanted to be abundantly successful so I could give to others without depriving myself.

One of the most rewarding programs I've been blessed to be a part of has been a platform we started for wounded warriors called Purple Heart Poetry. A Purple Heart veteran is a wounded warrior. It's a decoration earned through battle. I celebrate the fact that I am a Purple Heart veteran and am still alive to talk about it. The thing is, not every wounded warrior bears physical scars. Every single one of us is living with some kind of a wound. The battle has wounded all of us in some way.

I created Purple Heart Poetry in 2019 as a platform that would serve as a safe space for people to come together, share that story, and let it out—to take wounded thoughts and turn them into poetic words. What began as a program aimed at inviting poets, writers, and singers to share their stories soon became something else. Our gatherings grew until they were jam-packed with attendees, which provided us with an additional way to serve individuals at the practical and personal level.

At one Purple Heart Poetry event, I met a single working mother who didn't have transportation to get to work or take her kids to school. We decided to buy her a car. Another young lady hadn't seen her mom in years. We blessed her with a flight to go and reconnect with her mother. Another gentleman needed a vehicle to be able to provide for his family, so we blessed him with one. These are one of many stories of the impact that we had.

I don't share these stories for an applause; I share them to illustrate the fact that it all happened so organically. It wasn't really planned. It all just came from our why. Our goal was to help people. So eventually, we made it a policy. At every single event we did, we always chose someone whom we genuinely felt was in need of help that we could provide, and we did something to shift their life in a positive way.

The impact that we've had on the community of wounded warriors out there is astonishing to see. But truly, my biggest gain out of building that platform has been seeing people leave better than they came.

So, how about you?

If you pay attention, you'll start to hear these sorts of stories all around you. And if your antenna is up, if you are attuned, you'll start to see ways that you can help. You don't have to buy someone a car to change their life forever.

What advice would you give to someone considering entrepreneurship?

If you want love, give it first. If you want a connection, connect first. Be the outlet or be the plug. Most importantly, if you want hard work, be the hardest working person in the room.

There's nothing I ask of anybody else around me that I am not willing to do myself. From cleaning the toilets all the way up to making the difficult decisions that shift our companies' direction.

In the beginning of this chapter, I spoke of the daily chores we did back in Haiti to keep our family going. You had to grow up fast in an environment like that, even in a safe, tight-knit community like ours.

There's a scar on my hand that I have to this day. It dates back to my childhood, back to when even something as throwing out the trash meant a nice long walk. I remember that night like it was yesterday. The night sky glimmered with stars as my brother and I raced down the rocky hill below our house carrying the trash bags. In my zeal to win the race, I tripped on a rock and I fell, landing with my hand on top of one of the trash bags—a bag that contained broken glass. I remember looking down in shock at the split in my hand. Even in that meager light, I could see the red streaming out of it.

When I look at that scar today, it's a reminder of where I come from, the foundation my childhood set up for me, and how seemingly mundane, everyday tasks are still just as important as they were back then. There's nothing I ask of anyone around me, whether in business, the military, or my personal life that I'm not willing to do myself. No one who knows me would be surprised to see me get down on my knees to scrub the floor, then throw on a suit and go close a deal.

Be the first one in. Be the last one out. Never lose the humility to scrub the floor.

What is your ultimate impact?

If you've learned anything from this chapter, I hope it is an extension of the ultimate impact I hope to share with everyone around me: faith moves mountains.

Faith literally shapes the fabric of the universe around you. Today, you picked up this book. But you're reading the words that I wrote here because I spoke this into existence two years prior when I told my wife that we were going to be authors because the world needed to hear our stories. I didn't know the how behind it, and I didn't need to. If you have faith and put in the work, people will show up to make it happen.

It's my goal that after you close the book in this chapter, you will walk away with undeniable faith in yourself, the certainty that even when nobody else believes, you can get it done.

Faith is believing in the unseen—seeing things that are sometimes beyond our ability to comprehend. You may not know how you're going to reach this massive goal you've set for yourself. Leave that to God. That's how I have lived my whole life, and I promise you, it works. I've learned that when God tells me to move and I take that first step and walk in obedience and faith, He always puts the right people around me in order to bring everything to fruition. The rest of the world calls them coincidences, but like I already told you, I don't believe in coincidences. They're just God's way of remaining anonymous.

Start with faith and the how is none of your business.

I once read a quote that says, "when you set yourself on fire, people show up to watch you burn."

Thank you, Lord.

How can people connect with you?

I can be found at livluxwellness.com and on Instagram @SteveThelusma.

WITH PROPER ALIGNMENT,
WE HAVE A DIRECTION,
WITH A MUCH HIGHER
LEVEL OF IMPACT.

DK Warinner

CHAPTER 16

THE FEELING IS THE IMPACT
BY DK WARINNER

> **"I'VE LEARNED THAT PEOPLE WILL FORGET WHAT YOU SAID,
> PEOPLE WILL FORGET WHAT YOU DID, BUT PEOPLE WILL NEVER
> FORGET HOW YOU MADE THEM FEEL."**
>
> —*Maya Angelou*

Smile and nod with me if you can instantly recall a personal encounter that was important enough to remember, where you left it wondering how you made that special person feel? If you're thinking "Nah, that wasn't so important," then why do you remember it?

As I think of how I was led to become an impact entrepreneur, Maya Angelou's words suddenly have a more powerful meaning. They are not just an admonishment to be sensitive as we communicate or to govern our behavior in consideration of others. This principle and power impacts people in powerful and profound ways!

Some years ago, I was walking down a long hallway toward the secure access door of the business unit where I'd recently been assigned. Once I went through that door, I would become an operations strategy manager, or so I thought. My new boss came through the door and said curtly, "How was your trip?" I extended my hand for a handshake to connect and express appreciation for the new position and all of the opportunities it represented.

My new boss looked me over briefly, turned and went back through the door. My handshake was not returned! I brushed off the event, attempting to think nothing of it, but there was something in my gut that red-alerted. Something was wrong here! Unfortunately, that gesture was not just an impolite response but a representation of many similar events and a general feeling of unwelcomeness that overshadowed my entire experience there.

Although I was joining a new group, this was not a new employer for me. I had carefully built a career and reputation at the corporate office and the other business units (both large, multimillion-dollar businesses). The experience that unfolded at this new unit was nothing short of a disaster in my mind. I could see my investment, what I had built at this company, crumbling in front of my eyes, all because of the unsupportive (and, as it turned out, detrimental) position taken by the boss.

Sparing you the gory details, I learned a couple of key points through the experience:

1. I could be dismissed, regardless of how much I had invested.
2. All that I had built at the company could amount to nothing.

Sounds like hardcore Zen "no-mind" training, doesn't it? That's what it became for me. As I struggled to survive this experience (I had reasons at the time that kept me from departing immediately in search of something better), I came face to face with my deepest desires and my deepest fears. I realized that I had invested so heavily in my corporate career to build only that, a career, elevating me to a new position in that corporation where I would have impact.

A two-step approach.

First, invest. Learn the ropes. Do the work.

Second, deliver impact within the corporation.

What was I doing, then, while investing, learning, and doing the work? Supporting the impact of someone else or simply disappearing into the grand machine as a contributor.

What if other members of the corporation are uninterested or even politically opposed to me having an impact?

As I felt that opposition as a new member of this business unit, I realized that I was sowing into the wind, expending huge amounts of energy and effort to support a team that not only didn't support me in return, but parts of it were acting in quiet opposition to my work!

When I left that unit, one of my connections at HQ shared his perspective:

"You were in a no-win situation."

I'm glad I didn't spend more valuable years in that!

By leaving, I had started a new journey, where I transitioned from career-building to skills-building. Being in the right meetings, the right places at the right times gave way to moving more quickly between roles—finding insights to share and also build into a growing skill set. Several moves later, I had a much more diverse skill set and doubled the number of organizational cultures I had experienced.

I felt something was still missing. I saw the world of entrepreneurship through social media, where individuals were growing their businesses by leaps and bounds every month! What I noticed most of all was they were visible.

In a corporation, I would work a lot harder to be visible, and it would be, at best, a mix of my personal brand and the corporation's name. I did my research, slowly at first, until I found a few mentors and coaches who shined light into what needed to change the most:

Me

I could "make myself suitable" with advancing skills and earn my way forward.

Or I could get out of my own way and make an impact with what I already had!

The thought of this felt very, very good.

I learned a new set of skills that prepared me to remove obstacles, resistance, blocks to progress and open up new possibilities for the people I would serve.

I got out of my head and into my heart, speaking into the true desires of my colleagues, friends, and clients, awakening them to their potential.

Most of all, I tuned and aligned my own being from the inside out, finding that truth within all of us that doesn't ever change regardless of the circumstances, where even those circumstances will align to that truth. At first the evidence of this was small, coincidences here and there, until there was enough to build a bigger picture:

I had achieved impact.

Impact that didn't come from membership in a corporation or a track record of point-in-time accomplishments or activities.

Impact generated from simply being

The new me

I built a brand around my own inner struggle now won, and my first clients who came to me to resolve their feelings of high anxiety and panic at a crippling level:

The Center of Calmness.

As I observed what was happening as this new brand took shape, even as many people I knew didn't understand it or appreciate its value, I noticed a key impact:

People would tell me or share with others around me that I bring abundant calm wherever I am. People who didn't know I was building The Center of Calmness. People who didn't even know I had become an entrepreneur.

Impact

In a recent coaching call (yes, as a coach and mentor, I also receive a lot of coaching!), I was led down a path of exploring what I really wanted out of my relationship with a significant client, someone who I was investing a lot of time in.

As I went down the list of benefits I was supporting this client to produce, my coach kept asking,

What result does that bring?

And, what result does <u>that</u> bring?

And, what result does that bring?

Leading (not obvious to me, at the time) to the conclusive end result and the critical question:

How is this relationship supporting my reason for being in this world, my purpose?

This is my impact.

With this frame of mind, the feeling I have as I'm working with my client is different even while I'm dealing with the problems he's brought me to solve.

It's stronger and more positive.

It's appreciative, with gratitude.

It's solution oriented, coming from a place of being, not the rat race of endless doing.

As a result, changes are happening.

I'm having impact!

Along with this great feeling (within me and shared with my client), I've received clarity on how to keep the impact flowing to generate a feeling of true expansion:

Choice

Choice that started by my choosing how I would see my world—the outside world, as well as the world that is within.

Choice that continues by allowing myself to make specific choices about what I would like to create in my world.

Where I saw flexibility and the ability to change as important for surviving and thriving in a changing world, I now see the importance of creating and supporting specific and detailed choices as the way to generate measurable, meaningful, and lasting impact.

How?

It's in the feeling.

Flexibility and change generate a sense of freedom which is a sort of impact.

Committing to specific choices generates a sense of certainty and confidence.

Seeing those choices transition from vision to reality generates the confidence to make more choices and see them become reality, as well.

With proper alignment, we have a direction, with a much higher level of impact.

With this change in focus, The Center of Calmness transformed from a place of tranquility (supportive) to a place of motivation through clarity and focus (impactful), leading me to my choice to help corporate managers and entrepreneurs create impact by training their minds to act and react in a clear and focused way.

I create impact by helping others increase their level of impact!

People never forget how that makes them feel.

What is the "why" behind what you do?

So much of what I've seen in the past, both in myself and others, revolved around the expectations of others. As children, it was our parents and peers. As young adults, our society and schools shaped us. Early to mid-career, our companies and industry associations drove us. In late career, there's the fear of missing out before the window closes, keeping up with our image of success and our perception of what makes life enjoyable.

Where do our hearts come in? Where do we find the space to create a life of our own true nature and purpose?

What if we could create that life of our own design, whether we leverage the structure we've created at the workplace and our communities or choose to build something completely new, where we allow ourselves to fully express what we're about in a way that's powerful and impactful?

I impact the world through every person who, through my proven process, finds their way to the place where they create the life they love, without compromise.

What unique framework or service do you offer to your community or clients?

I offer my clients mentorship, coaching, and consulting to significantly increase their level of impact professionally and personally, through a superconscious creative framework that positions and differentiates them for impact.

How were you able to transform a setback into a setup for success?

In my story above, I mentioned the corporate gig that woke me up to entrepreneurship and impact through transforming lives, as measured by my traditional career lens. The way that gig turned out was definitely a setback. I spent years building a new branch of my career journey that was much less dependent on the corporations I associated with, positioning me as more personally impactful as I approach new situations from the standpoint of skill set and contribution. The political quagmire that got me out, actually got me into entrepreneurship!

What role do collaboration and community have in your business?

I have a very high sense of gratitude for the communities I've been blessed with on this journey: people working together with different goals and objectives and a common mindset, a common striving and driving for the kind of progress that leads to lasting success. I'm inspired daily by fellow mentors and coaches who share key insights and spur me along to be, do, and have greater than what I see possible in myself!

My coaching and mentorship includes community development and leverage so that I can continue sharing the benefits I've received through deep collaboration. Each of us has unique strengths and challenges, and we move farther and faster together, without diluting the uniqueness of who we are and what we offer, by sharing and receiving in community.

What life or business lessons have created the most growth for you?

The most powerful realization I've found is that almost nothing is really new. It's our interpretation of first principle and wisdom as expressed through our own personal lens that delivers something old or forgotten in a fresh, new way that is impactful to our audiences. Realizing this let me off the hook and allowed me to release too high standards and perfectionism to get out there and contribute.

Along with this truth, I've realized that almost all of what holds us back is created within ourselves, our limiting beliefs that create a small box for us to live in. It can feel a little scary out there, where the rules might not be obvious and the potential is virtually unlimited! An amazing shift took place in me when I accepted the truth of creating my own limiting beliefs. Once I could see those beliefs for what they were, they became much easier and less painful to overcome.

In the end, it's about the choice we're making. Allow that to be and the path to get there will appear!

What advice would you give to someone considering entrepreneurship?

Get started early without thinking about it too much, keeping three things in mind.

First, passion. Do you truly love the business you're creating with all your heart? Why? What do you love about it? If you don't love it, it will be a lot harder to pour the effort and energy into it long term. Also, the business might not pay off as quickly as you think it will. There must be something within you that's willing to continue until your vision of that business becomes reality.

Second, profit. Does your business idea make money? Mentors and coaches can be very supportive here. Is there a market waiting for you? Will they be able to distinguish you from the crowd? Can they pay for your product, service, or support? Why would they want to—what do they get?

Third, plan. How will you deliver value? How will you get paid? How much revenue do you need to have to commit fully to the business? What are the numbers that get you to that revenue level? How many businesses or revenue streams are you planning to direct simultaneously? Who's on your support team?

Above all, find a client and serve them—give them value and let that experience inform your path forward. And don't forget to have them pay you for what you're doing for them!

What is your ultimate impact?

I envision The Center of Calmness as an internationally impactful brand embracing life to the fullest by leveraging inner peace, without accumulating the stress that often comes with pursuing success. I've fulfilled my mission when stressed professionals and entrepreneurs realize it doesn't have to be that way. They have a calmness within that provides access to limitless potential and more success than they were striving for under stress.

I envision leading a large community, where superconscious professionals and entrepreneurs accomplish a lot together as we effortlessly apply creative principles to impact millions.

How can people connect with you?

I can be found at dkwarinner.com and on Facebook @dk.warinner.

AS AN ENTREPRENEUR BE PREPARED TO WORK HARDER THAN YOU EVER HAVE BEFORE.

Harry Weiss

CHAPTER 17

SEVEN WEEKS CHANGED MY LIFE
BY HARRY WEISS

When I decided to write about entrepreneurship, I had to look up what an entrepreneur was. I wasn't really sure. *Webster's Dictionary* says one who creates and invests in a business. When I was growing up, that was called being self-employed, but either way that was never what I had in mind as a young man. I didn't need to get rich. I just didn't want a boss.

It was 1970, I was 23 years old, married, a college dropout, and just fired from my third job. To make matters worse, my last job was with my father, but I wasn't about to give up. Twelve years later I would be a multi-millionaire.

I went to an employment service, and they arranged for me to interview with a company selling wholesale popcorn. After two interviews, they told me they hired somebody else because the other person had a college degree. I couldn't believe it. I couldn't even get a job selling popcorn, but I did learn something else. I needed a college degree, so I went back and eighteen months later I had a piece of paper in my hand, a job at Mattel toy company selling Barbie dolls, and of course, Mattel only hires college graduates. Lucky me, I spent a year with Mattel and another year with Coleco, and six years as a buyer for Boscov's department stores.

I was actually a good buyer and thought it was the time to ask my boss, Mr. Boscov for a raise, or I would have to quit. He agreed that I was a good buyer but couldn't give me a raise and told me not to let the door hit me on the ass on the way out. So there I was, out of work again, but this time there was a big difference. I now knew something. I knew about toys. I knew how to buy them. I also knew how to sell them and thought maybe it was time to go into business for myself.

Location, location, location. If you want to be in a real estate business or for that matter any business, location is the key and of course, a little bit of luck. Well, maybe a lot of luck. So as far as location was concerned, at that time of my life, I was living in Reading, Pennsylvania. Reading was known as the factory outlet capital of the world. Now, of course, factory outlets are everywhere. If you're riding on I-95, it seems that every six exits is an outlet center, but back in the days of the '70s and '80s, Reading had the only outlets in the world. And I was living right there. Strangely enough, Reading had no toy outlet. They had men's clothes, women's clothes, and children's clothes, but no toy outlet. Vanity Fair had most of the outlets. Tommy Hilfiger, Izod, Levi jeans, Nike shoes, and everything else, but no toys! And they weren't going to have toys because the people in charge of Vanity Fair basically laughed at me, and they were right.

I was a nobody. They had national brands. I wasn't even a local brand. So I moved on to my second choice, and they also turned me down. Last but not least, I tried the big mill outlet. It just so happened the man who owned the big mill, Henry Halbesen, hated Mr. Boscov. He thought it was funny that one of Boscov's buyers wanted to compete against them, so he let me come in, although he adamantly would not give me a lease. He made it very clear that he would throw me out if he didn't like me, and I too could leave anytime I wanted. I ended up there for seven years.

So now I had a location, but that's it. I didn't have any fixtures. I didn't have any employees; I didn't have a cash register, and I didn't have any money. And I had no idea how to get any of those things. Don't forget, I was a toy buyer. That was it. I didn't know about finance. I didn't know about the operational side of it. All I knew was if I could buy it at the right price, I could sell it at the right price. So my first task was to get a line of credit.

As luck would have it, I had a drinking buddy named Nelson who mentioned he was a banker. I often thought it hard to believe because many nights I had to carry him out of the bar. So I called Nelson and told him what I wanted to do. He invited me to come into his office. Bingo! Right on his office door, there it was: Vice President of Business Loans. So we discussed tennis and women just like we did at the bar we hung out in. Then I decided it was time to bring up business. When I started to pitch him, he said, "Harry, don't bother, you can have anything you want." Sometimes it pays off to have an extra martini.

Next, I had to visit my vendors. Well, not my vendors but my former employer's vendors. Everyone, without exception, gave me a small line of credit: $10,000 here, $5,000 there. The man, Dave, I was counting on the most, turned me down. I was shocked. He was my mentor. This was the man who taught me about toys. He saw the disappointment on my face and then told me, "I won't just give $10,000. I'll give you unlimited credit." In addition, one of my vendors in Miami, Carlos, gave me $25,000 in credit. When I was about to leave his office, he took out a gun and said, "You better pay me back, or I'm coming after you." He was the first one I paid back.

Wow, I was on my way. Next, I needed a store manager. I had no experience at that level, so I did the smart thing and hired a woman named Mickey, who had even less experience. I thought she was honest and hard-working and she needed a job, so now we were a team.

The third thing I needed were store fixtures. When you walk into a department store or any store, you really don't notice what the merchandise is sitting on, but if you have no shelving, the merchandise sits on the floor, and that's not a good way to sell. So I decided to go out and look for fixtures, not realizing how expensive they were. "What did I get myself into," I asked.

But as luck would have it, the Litt brothers of Philadelphia went bankrupt and were selling off all their stores, fixtures and office furniture, and many other things I could use. So with a rented truck, off I went to Philadelphia. They had everything I needed, all the way down to file folders. I bought what I thought I needed and paid somewhere in the vicinity of ten cents on the dollar. It took me about two weeks to put it all together and now we had a store. It wasn't Bloomingdale's, for that matter; it wasn't even Kmart, but it went along with our motto: "We're not fancy, but we're cheap."

It would help a lot if we had some merchandise to put on the shelves, so there I was off on a buying trip. It was a little different now, for one thing I was buying much smaller quantities than when I was at Boscov's, yet I was asking for the same discounts. Where before I was buying at least two gross of an item, now I'm buying just a dozen pieces. But they went along with me and gave me the prices that I needed. I knew that wouldn't last forever, but the good news was my shelves were now full, and I was ready to open.

I then ran a small ad in the local newspaper and gave away free hotdogs. The people came, nothing crazy, but a good sign that things were headed to a bright future. For the first three months—August, September, and October—we had some nice sales, and we actually made a small profit, which is pretty cool when you've only been in business for three months.

Now it was time for Oklahoma. I spent most of my time on the telephone looking for merchandise at an advantageous price. I used to call all the toy wholesalers across the country seeing if they had excess inventory to sell as well as manufacturers' closeouts. The problem with manufacturers is I really couldn't buy enough to make it worthwhile for them, but with a small wholesaler, they were happy to sell me what I needed. I was talking to a friend of mine who ran a wholesale company in Cincinnati. He informed me that a large wholesaler in Oklahoma City was going out of business,

Farah Distributors, so I gave them a call. I told them who I was and mentioned what I wanted to do, and they told me to come out.

The next day I hopped on a plane and flew to Oklahoma City. The person I spoke to there was JC Livingstone; he was the man in charge of the liquidation and was supposed to meet me at the Holiday Inn that morning for breakfast. I kept walking around asking people, "Dr. Livingstone, I presume?" They all answered no and for good reason. He was not there; he never showed up. I was off to a good start, so I called JC and he apologized and sent one of his guys to come pick me up. When I got to the office, he shook my hand and put me with a salesman. He quoted me a price, and I countered with a lower price. The answer was always no. However, he did say he would negotiate, but in the end he didn't, and after 45 minutes I walked out wasting a lot of time and money which I didn't have.

But again, as luck would have it, I had a girlfriend who lived in Houston, Texas that I hadn't seen for a while, so I decided to jump down there for a couple days before heading back to Reading, Pennsylvania. I needed some R&R. I'd been working pretty hard the last few months. When I got there, I called my office, and my store manager, Mickey, informed me that JC Livingston called and wanted to talk to me. I wasn't too happy about the situation. I really didn't want to talk to JC, but I did. He apologized and told me to come back, and he would make it worth my while. So I did.

If I hadn't flown to Houston first to see my girlfriend, there was no way I would've gone back to Oklahoma City. Since I was already in Houston, I thought, why not? I was going to do it differently this time. As soon as I landed, JC was there to meet me. On the way from the airport I suggested we stop by the cowboy store and buy boots. He took me to his favorite store, and encouraged me to buy a cowboy hat. Of course, the one he pointed out was made of mink and cost a lot of money, but I bought it anyway just to make an impression.

Now I was ready. I had my boots, I had my hat, and all I needed now was a six shooter and I was a full-blown cowboy. Well, I think I'll pass on the six shooter, but it was time to go to work, and now it was me and JC. It turned out to be a very profitable afternoon, and when I left, I thanked JC and his controller because she gave me a credit line without the need for any references. I did notice, however, that JC and Miss Della, the controller, were very friendly, so at the airport, I found a florist and sent her a dozen roses.

When I got back home to Reading, as soon as I walked in the door, the phone was ringing. It was JC. He wanted to thank me for the roses and told me if I came back out again, I would be very happy, and happy he did make me. I turned right around. I stayed there for almost a week. We worked all day and played all night, JC, myself, and Miss Della. I even learned how to two-step.

When I walked out of there, I had bought 2.5 million dollars of toys for $600,000 which equated to twenty-four cents on a dollar. What a deal. The only problem was I couldn't pay for it. Of course, they didn't know that. I knew that the bank wasn't gonna give me $600,000, so I had to find another solution.

Discount Harry to the rescue. No not me, but there was a store in New Jersey called Discount Harry, and we used to do a lot of business together, and they had a lot of money, so I made him a deal. I offered to give them half the inventory if they would pay for the whole thing. I said I would pay them back when I could. It was a win-win for everybody.

Now I own 2.5 million dollars of toys. I'm doing about $30,000 a week in business, and I have seven weeks until Christmas to sell the toys. By the way, 2.5 million dollars translates into thirty 40 foot tractor trailers of merchandise. I have a store that's 2800 ft.² and a stock room of 2000 ft.², and about a half a dozen employees. Now it's time to go to work.

The first thing I did was negotiate 10,000 ft.² of temporary warehouse space. I put together my advertising, featuring newspapers, radio, and television. As far as the store operations were concerned, I left hiring people to Dinah. She was the best. Dinah worked for me as a department manager when I was a buyer at Boscov's. A couple of months after I opened the store, she came in and told me she needed a job and that Boscov's fired her. It seemed that her merchandise manager's wife came in asking for something that was out of stock. She wasn't happy with the answer and was rude, so Dinah told her to go f**k herself. That was Dinah's last day at Boscov's. My only problem was I already had a manager and couldn't afford a new person, but Dinah said she would work for nothing. How could I turn her down? She didn't want to stay home. She hated her husband and wanted to work. Now we had a full team.

So now we had to move the toys as fast as possible. Every day a tractor trailer arrived delivering toys from Oklahoma City to our outlet center. I put together an aggressive advertising plan to move the merchandise as fast as possible before the next truck arrived. It was working perfectly until one day the truck broke down and arrived late. We had a full page ad of Star Wars toys and no merchandise to sell. We had hundreds of people waiting outside for the toys at half price. One hour later, the truck finally arrived with no time to unload, so we just stood by the back of the truck and grabbed the merchandise and threw it to the customers hoping they would go inside and pay for it. The people were thrilled to get brand-new Star Wars toys at half price.

We were now doing well into six figures a week. We increased our hours from 9:00 am to 9:00 pm every day and 10:00 am to 5:00 pm on Sunday. On Christmas Day, we closed the store for the first time in two months. All the toys were sold! I took my key people to Puerto Rico for a well-deserved vacation.

Over the next couple of years I opened three more stores. All of them within a few blocks from each other. I did that because we were in the outlet business, and we used to bus people in from out of town, and they had only so many hours to shop. By having three stores they had to hit at least one of them, and besides it kept out the competition.

Unfortunately, seven years after I opened the first store, the building was sold to a real estate company from New York City. They were not satisfied with the rent I was paying and approached me with a lease agreement. Remember, I had never had a lease before.

Initially, I opened the store paying $3.50 per square foot, and after seven years, it had increased to about eight dollars per square foot. The New York real estate company deemed this unacceptable and proposed a five-year lease at $25 per square foot, with a 10 percent annual increase. Sadly, I had to bid farewell to the original store. Three years later, at the age of 43, I decided to retire and consequently closed all the stores.

What life or business lessons have created the most growth for you?

If you asked me today how to become an entrepreneur, I would suggest following my path. At the time, I didn't know what I was doing, but in hindsight, it seems much easier. Firstly, attend college. The primary reason is the lifelong friendships you'll make, which can open doors both personally and professionally. Secondly, a degree enables you to work at a Fortune 500 company, where you can receive excellent training and build valuable relationships. Ensure you have financial resources, either in savings or access to credit. And remember, whatever resources you have may not be enough. Lastly, be prepared to work harder than you ever have before. With these steps, you're ready to begin. Good luck!

What is your ultimate impact?

My ultimate goal is to have the freedom to enjoy my life and engage in activities that have always been important to me. As a single father with full custody of my daughter since she was five, I managed to retire when she turned fourteen. Retirement gave me the flexibility to dedicate myself to my daughter, Kim, particularly to her passion for basketball. Being present at her games, encouraging her during practices, and supporting her love for the sport led to her earning a full basketball scholarship in college. She also became a highly successful entrepreneur, and we remain close to this day.

How can people connect with you?

I can be found at pgaboca@hotmail.com and on Instagram @HarryWeiss.

CONCLUSION

Dear Current or Future Impact-preneur,

We want to leave you with this final thought … every single one of us has the unique ability to impact others. It starts with a clear vision and recognizing you can do anything that you deeply care about and are driven to pursue. Consider this book as a compass that will guide you through the challenges and learning curve that come during the start-up phase. Remember, every author here started at ground zero.

Once your business is up and running, the community you build and the impact you have on others will lead you the rest of the way. Remember, you are not alone, and you've got this. Also, remember to pause and celebrate your wins, even the small ones. Doing so will give you the fuel to keep going when times are tough. It's an incredible journey and truly fulfilling, but there will be days where it's hard. The impact you are making will keep you going.

If you need help getting started, know we are always there to support you.

Along the way, we encourage you to collaborate with others. Entrepreneurship can be lonely if you try to go it alone, or it can be enriching and exciting when shared with world-changing people like yourself. This book is evidence of what happens when impact-driven business owners come together to share their stories.

What you don't see are the Zoom calls and private WhatsApp group, where we support each other's events, launches, and businesses. You aren't privy to the brand-building photo shoot, speaking events, and masterminding that ensures that each one of these best-selling authors feels supported as they scale their businesses. It's about the collective coming together for the highest, greatest good of all.

In writing this book together, we've become friends, collaborators, and cheerleaders for each other. As a reader, we personally invite you to join us in community as we continue to build and grow together. Follow and engage with the authors who resonated most with you, invite them on your podcasts, mention them in an Amazon review, and reach out to us if you are interested in joining us in future projects. We'd love to hear from you.

To your success,

Wendi & Patricia

JOIN US IN THE UNLEASH ACADEMY

About the Unleash Academy

Our Academy was created to help experts (just like you) brand themselves as authorities in their field within a community of supportive entrepreneurs.

We know it's not easy to build your foundation, whether it's a best-selling book, speaking, digital courses, or coaching while trying to network and do everything it takes to get your name out there. Our goal is to help you build your assets, which is why every month we tackle a new theme with a workshop to complete a project. In addition, we host monthly networking and member presentations so we can grow our businesses together as a community.

To learn more, visit:
https://www.woostermediabooks.com/academy

ABOUT THE AUTHORS

WENDI BLUM WEISS

Wendi is the founder of The Speakers and Coaches Networking Society, an international audience of 18K+, where she provides education, resources, and support to help hundreds of purpose-driven entrepreneurs amplify their voices, reach more people, and elevate their impact.

As a podcast host, published author of seven books, and an international speaker, she has spoken on college campuses, taught courses around the world, led international retreats, and hosted masterminds on topics that combine elevating your energy and harnessing your brilliance as it pertains to creativity, productivity, health optimization, and business success.

In 2022, Wendi joined forces with Patricia Wooster to empower entrepreneurs to stand out in a crowded marketplace by building their own audience, community, and brand through becoming best-selling authors, speaking on stages, and evolving their brand into a trusted authority. They bring together the best of entrepreneurial wisdom, energy tools, and community to help more people unleash their greatness, both personally and professionally.

PATRICIA WOOSTER

Patricia is the founder of WoosterMedia Publishing, where she helps experts, executives, and entrepreneurs codify their wisdom and leverage their expertise into books, digital courses, workshops, speeches, consulting, and media opportunities. Her clients include C-level executives, college professors, professional athletes, and media personalities who have landed agents, major publishing contracts, speaking opportunities, and best-seller status.

She is the author of 19 books, including the award-winning and best-selling *Ignite Your Spark* with Simon & Schuster, and three entrepreneur co-author books with Wendi Blum Weiss. Her experience ranges from working with companies and organizations like Disney, Home Shopping Network, WeDay, Informix Software, Designing Genius, and KPMG to working with start-up entrepreneurs and influencers.

Today, she is partnered with Wendi Blum Weiss to teach entrepreneurs how to successfully brand themselves as best-selling authors, speakers, and experts in their field. As creators of the Encore Expert Academy, they teach entrepreneurs how to create clarity and confidence around their personal brand and core strengths while building a strong foundation of assets that create credibility and amazing opportunities.

In addition to helping people unleash their superpowers, Patricia and Wendi are passionate about teaching entrepreneurs how to leverage their energy through functional health practices and the newest biohacking protocols to increase performance and creativity. They believe the key to a purpose-driven life is optimizing physical vitality and mindfulness and empowering entrepreneurs to establish themselves as influential thought leaders while prioritizing their well-being.

LEAVE A REVIEW

Before you go, if you enjoyed this book, will you please consider leaving a review on Amazon? As authors, there is nothing we appreciate more than reading reviews on Amazon and other bookseller websites from those who have enjoyed the book.

Thank you so much!
Wendi Blum Weiss & Patricia Wooster

Made in the USA
Middletown, DE
27 May 2024

54775994R00130